Fun Figures

CUTE CHARACTER CAKE TOPPERS FOR ALL OCCASIONS

DEDICATION

To my parents, Anne and John Duffy,
with love.

Fun Figures

CUTE CHARACTER CAKE TOPPERS
FOR ALL OCCASIONS

LORRAINE MCKAY

SEARCH PRESS

ACKNOWLEDGEMENTS

Special thanks and much love to Kyla Myers. You have been with me on an incredible journey and your friendship knows no bounds. I thank you for keeping my spirits up and for feeding me – literally! – throughout this long process. I appreciate you more than I can say.

Thanks to my girls, Vicky and Claire, for your support and encouragement every day.

To Luci, my sugar friend always. To my Facebook Mafia! Without your following and support this book would not be possible. To Diane at Renshaw, for providing me with all I need at the drop of a hat! I appreciate it. To Poppy, my faithful, furry and often distracting companion.

Big hugs and thanks to my grandchildren. You fill me with inspiration every day. I love you.

First published in 2015

Search Press Limited
Wellwood, North Farm Road,
Tunbridge Wells, Kent TN2 3DR

Illustrations and text copyright © Lorraine McKay 2015

Photographs by Paul Bricknell at Search Press Studio

Photographs and design copyright © Search Press Ltd 2015

ISBN: 978-1-78221-032-0

The Publishers and author can accept no responsibility for any consequences arising from the information, advice or instructions given in this publication.

Suppliers
If you have difficulty in obtaining any of the materials and equipment mentioned in this book, then please visit the Search Press website for details of suppliers: www.searchpress.com

You are invited to visit the author's website: www.extraicing.co.uk

Printed in China

Contents

Introduction

If anyone had suggested to me a few years ago that I would be decorating cakes, far less writing a book about it, I would have laughed out loud! But here I am today, not only a cake decorator, but a tutor who travels around the world demonstrating my skills to anyone who cares to take notice.

This hobby of mine began in 2003, when I discovered the world of sugar. I have always been an artistic person with a keen interest in all things animated, and nothing cheers me more than seeing a cute cartoon figure with a heap of character. With a keen sense of humour and an eye for detail, I discovered that I had a hidden talent. Making sugar figures and creating expression became my passion.

With no paper qualification for this kind of thing, I entered my novel cake designs in the competitions at the International Cake Show in Birmingham. I now have several Gold Certificates to my name and have gone on from there to become an Accredited Demonstrator for the British Sugarcraft Guild. This takes me around various venues up and down the country, where I demonstrate my skills with figure modelling to an enthusiastic audience. I make the most of this opportunity and entertain the crowd with my humour, which comes in handy, as things don't always go according to plan! To come from nowhere and be recognised with such high regard in this amazing industry is quite an incredible experience. The time seems right to get my work in print and be proud of all that I have achieved. I have had an incredible journey thus far and I have no doubt there is much more to come. I hope this book inspires you to reach your goals and discover skills you never thought you had. Creativity is in all of us in some shape or form. Enjoy it!

Materials and tools

MODELLING MATERIALS

Fondant (sugarpaste)

Fondant (sugarpaste) is available in a variety of rich and vibrant ready-made colours, but with a bit of time and effort you can easily create tailor-made shades to suit your projects by mixing white fondant (sugarpaste) with colouring pastes. I used both methods for the projects in this book. I chose ready-made colours for the strongest of colours, like red and black, for example, but mixed my own flesh tones and more delicate shades.

CMC (tylose) powder

CMC (carboxymethyl cellulose, or tylose) is a gum powder that is added to fondant (sugarpaste) to make it more pliable and easy to use. It strengthens the paste so that your models will maintain their shape as the paste hardens. It can also be used to make edible glue.

Gum paste (flower paste)

Gum paste (flower paste) can be rolled out extremely thinly and is good for flower-making and also for creating other structures that would benefit from its additional strength. Gum paste (flower paste) already has enough elasticity for immediate use and does not require the addition of gum powder. The paste should be coloured in the same way that fondant (sugarpaste) is coloured. I used it to make the key for the 21st birthday project in this book. Left to dry overnight, your structures will be stronger than if made from modelling paste.

MODELLING PASTE RECIPE

To make 500g (1lb 1oz) of modelling paste, sprinkle 1 tsp of CMC (tylose) powder onto your work surface.

Knead the fondant (sugarpaste) into the powder until it is all well incorporated.

Store the modelling paste in an airtight bag.

SUGAR GLUE RECIPE

Into a container put one ¼ tsp of CMC (tylose) gum powder and add 2 tbsp of warm water. Place the lid tightly onto the container and shake. At this point, the powder will appear not to blend with the water and will look very lumpy. Place the container in the fridge and leave overnight. In the morning the glue will be perfectly clear and ready to use. The consistency should be like syrup. If the glue is too thick, gradually add warm water and stir until the correct consistency is reached.

COLOURING EQUIPMENT

Paintbrushes

I recommend using good-quality paintbrushes for gluing, painting and dusting. I use sable brushes as they last well and don't shed their hair. The brushes come in varying sizes: the smallest are ideal for adding fine detail, such as eyelashes, while the larger, rounded brushes are useful for gluing and other paintwork. The handles of the brushes come in pretty handy too, for opening sleeve ends and adding detail.

Dusting brush

A flat dusting brush is used for highlighting areas of your work with coloured dust powders. I also use a clean flat brush as an alternative 'finger'. In areas of work where a little adjustment is required, a flat brush will do the job with minimal fuss and less distortion. I use this in particular when placing the brides' dresses in position, as you will see in the wedding projects (see pages 103 and 116).

Paste and dust colours

Concentrated colours are added to fondant (sugarpaste) gradually until the depth of colour required is achieved. Mix colours together to create something new. Powder colours can be used to enhance areas of projects by dusting with a flat brush. Both paste and dust colours can be mixed with a little alcohol and used for painting.

Food-grade alcohol

Clear alcohol is used to mix powder and paste colours to a painting consistency. Vodka or gin are my preferred choices. Rejuvenator spirit, which can be found in craft stores, is often used for this purpose but it is a little more expensive.

Confectioner's glaze

This is used to add shine to elements of the design. It is used in the confectionery industry as a coating on boiled sweets. I use it to shine shoes and eyes on the models. Used with lustre powders it creates a varnish. Thoroughly clean the brush you use for this purpose in isopropyl alcohol and cold water after use.

OTHER EQUIPMENT

Corn flour (corn starch)

This is used to dust the work surface, and your hands if necessary, to prevent the paste from sticking.

Small scissors

These are particularly useful when dressing your models and for making adjustments to paste while it is in place. They may also be used for texturing and hairstyling.

Plastic ball tool

This is used to hollow or indent the paste.

Metal ball tool

This does the same as any other ball tool but gives a smoother finish. Choose the size of ball to suit the task.

Scriber needle

This is primarily used for scribing patterns onto cakes before piping a design with royal icing. I use it to create fine detail on sugar clothing.

Designer wheel

This is available with changeable wheels – the varying wheels are used to add design detail to your work.

Quilting and stitching wheel

The small stitching wheel is excellent for creating seams and designs on the clothing of the models. The wheel is small enough to use directly on the model, allowing you to create some of the design after the clothing is in place.

Cutting wheel

A cutting tool with different sized wheels, this is used to cut small sugar shapes.

Bone tool

The bone tool is used to make indents and to smooth and stretch the paste without tearing it.

Plastic leaf veiner

This tool is useful for adding texture. The larger and slightly rounded end of the tool is also excellent for creating wide, smiling mouths for your figures.

Metal leaf veiner

This has the same use as the plastic version but gives a smoother and cleaner finish – the sharp end will cut into the paste without leaving a ragged edge, which makes shaping a lot easier. It is also ideal for creating mouths.

Small rolling pin

Used for rolling out paste.

Knife

A good-quality craft knife with a fine blade is essential for creating a clean edge when cutting straight lines or shapes in the paste.

Polystyrene mould

A small round polystyrene mould is excellent for holding heads in place while you work on the facial detail. It will help to keep the head's rounded shape and prevent distortion from warm fingers.

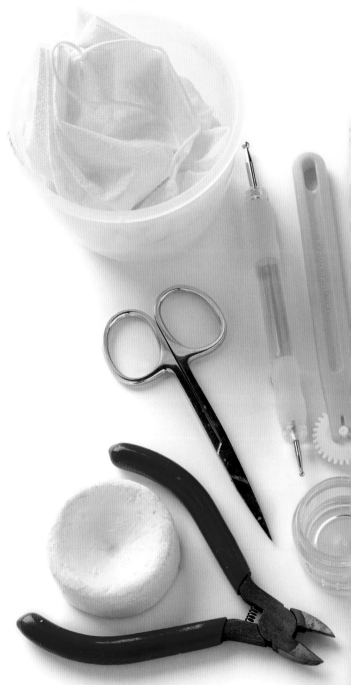

Glue

Edible glue is essential for sticking pieces of paste together. Ready-made edible glue is available in craft stores but it is much more economical to make your own (see page 8). For the best results, the glued area should be tacky to the touch and not wet. Use a fine paintbrush to apply your glue accurately.

Piping tips and cutters

Use an assortment of cutters to create basic small shapes. As well as cutting mini flowers to enhance your designs, floral cutters can also be used to emboss paste. Piping tips can also be used to add detail.

Sponge

Cut to size and use to support parts of the model that require overnight drying.

Measuring spoon

Used to measure the correct quantity of CMC (tylose) powder to strengthen fondant (sugarpaste, see page 8).

Cocktail and kebab sticks

Cocktail sticks are used to add colour to your paste and may also be used as supports. Kebab sticks are cut to size and used as supports for heavier figures.

Snippers

Used to trim wooden supports safely and easily.

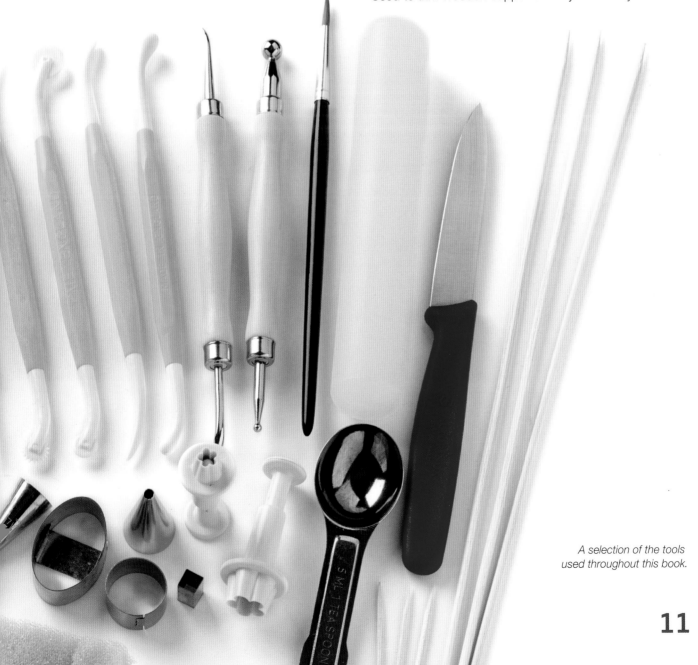

A selection of the tools used throughout this book.

Techniques

MAKING A HEAD

The amount of paste you'll need to make a head will depend on the size of the model. You will make the body first and then the head will be proportioned to suit. The weights given in each project should be used as a guide only. The techniques used for shaping a head are the same for each model; size, paintwork and a little additional detail will determine the age, gender and expression.

Shaping the head

Knead the paste to warm it then roll it into a smooth, round ball.

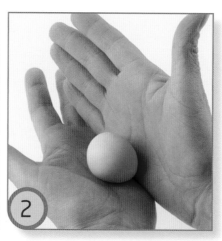

Roll the ball into a cone shape using your palms as shown.

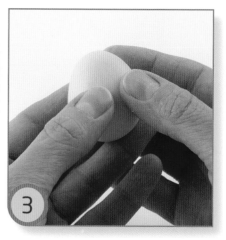

Flatten one side of the cone slightly to create the face.

Support the face while gradually pinching the paste at the wide end of the cone until there is enough to grasp between your finger and thumb.

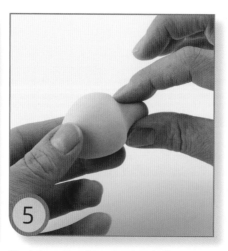

Pinch from the sides, front and all around in little movements until the neck lengthens.

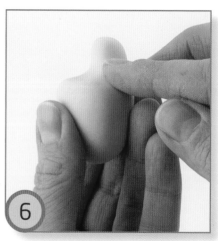

Smooth away any unwanted lines under the chin with the tips of your fingers.

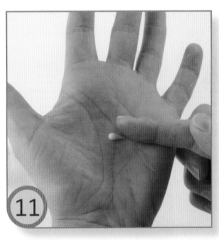

Pinch the cheeks in a downward motion to shape and smooth.

Gently pinch the chin between your thumbs to shape.

Adding a nose

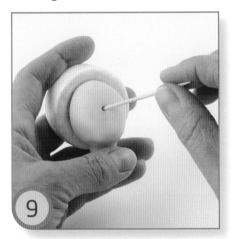

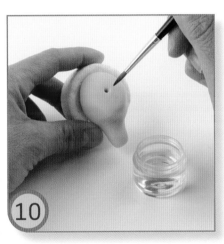

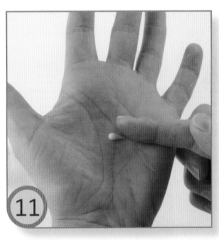

Place the head in a polystyrene mould and use a cocktail stick to make a hole, twisting gently to widen slightly.

Using a paintbrush, insert glue in the hole before making the nose. Don't add too much or it will seep out when the nose is inserted.

Roll a tiny teardrop shape using paste of the same colour as the head.

Insert the pointed end into the hole and flatten a little with your finger.

Using a tiny ball tool, create two nostrils. Smooth the inside of each nostril with soft strokes. Make a final adjustment if necessary to reshape the face before continuing to add further detail.

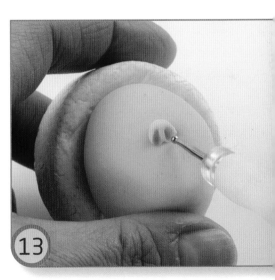

13

Shaping the cheekbones

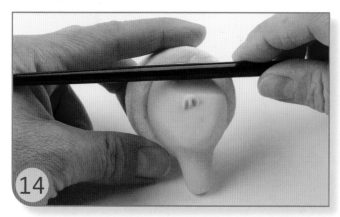

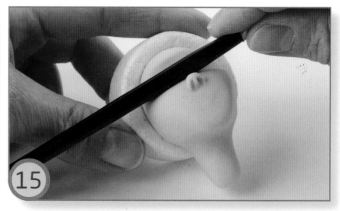

Roll a paintbrush handle across the top of the nose to create the cheekbones. Keeping the handle in a horizontal line, push down firmly on one side and carefully roll the handle upwards with a little less pressure.

Repeat the step on the other side. Smooth across the indent and the sides of the eye area with the tip of your finger. Continue to smooth and readjust the shape of the head as you work each detail.

Cutting and smoothing the mouth

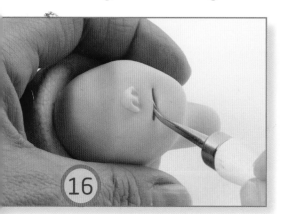

Use the sharp end of the leaf veiner to create a mouth. Push the tool into each corner and gently sweep towards the centre. Do this once or twice, deepening the groove with slight movements each time.

Use the rounded end of the leaf veining tool to push gently into the centre of the mouth. Shape the bottom lip by supporting it underneath with a thumb while pulling the paste down and outwards against it with the veining tool. Work around the mouth in this manner until the bottom lip is smooth and protruding slightly.

Indent the corners of the mouth with a small ball tool.

To create the top lip, place the rounded end of the veiner, with the scooped side facing upward, into the mouth and gently pull out the top lip.

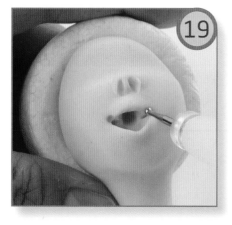

Make a little dimple on the top lip using the small ball tool.

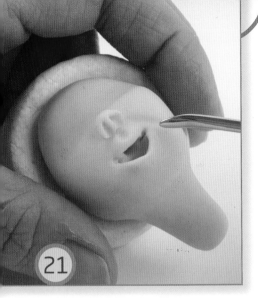

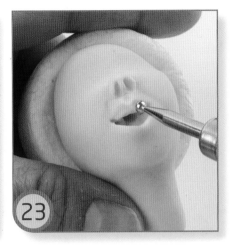

21

With gentle pressure, use the rounded end of the leaf veiner to highlight the cheeks using diagonal strokes from the outside of each nostril to the corners of the mouth.

22

Reshape and smooth from the cheeks towards the chin and towards the back of the head to redefine and eliminate any unwanted lines.

23

To create the top lip, use the small ball tool as if applying lipstick. Stroke the paste from the centre of the top lip and taper off to each corner. The lip will thicken a little as you create it, so tap against the inside of the top lip in an upward motion, until it thins as required.

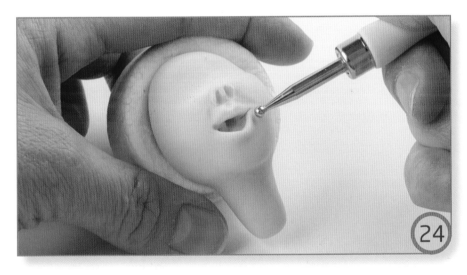

24

Bring the corners of the mouth together, gently sweeping in a downward direction from the top lip towards each outer corner and repeating the same along the bottom lip towards each corner.

Making eye sockets

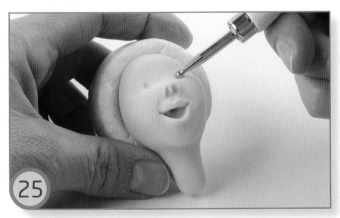

25

Taking care to space them evenly, indent the centre of each eye socket using the small ball tool.

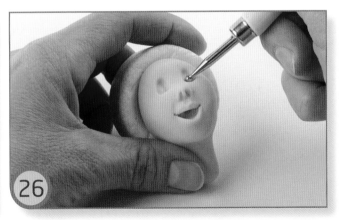

26

Using small circular movements, create a wider hollow for each eye socket.

Colouring the cheeks

Blend a tiny amount of rose powder colour with icing (powdered) sugar. This will soften the tone of the colour and also allow you to apply it gradually until the right amount of blush is reached. Stroke it onto the cheeks using a broad, soft paintbrush.

Making teeth

28

29

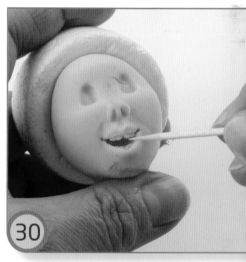

30

Apply glue to the inside of the bottom lip and on the underside of the top lip. Roll two tiny pieces of white fondant (sugarpaste) into a sausage. The bottom teeth will barely be noticeable and should be much smaller in size than the top teeth.

Position the teeth with a cocktail stick, pushing it into the centre to ensure the pastes have adhered.

Tap along the tiny strips with the point of the cocktail stick to create indents for the individual teeth.

Creating eyeballs

Roll two tiny white balls of fondant (sugarpaste) to fit into each eye socket. Glue in position and smooth flat with a medium ball tool. The white of the eye should fit neatly into each socket and appear smooth and level around the eye area.

31

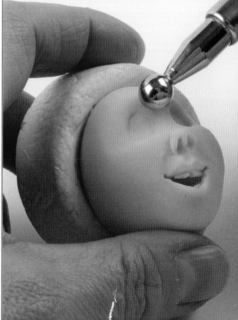

Adding fine detail

32 Mix a little dark brown paste colouring with a few drops of alcohol, until a smooth consistency is reached.

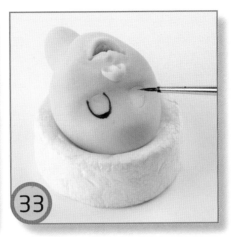

33 Paint around the outside of the eye using a fine paintbrush. I find this easier to do with the head upside down. Find the way that suits you best and use your work surface to support your hands.

34 Add a few eyelashes.

35 Paint on the eyebrows.

36 Roll two tiny black balls. Apply glue to the whites of the eyes using the tip of the paintbrush, taking care not to touch the paintwork.

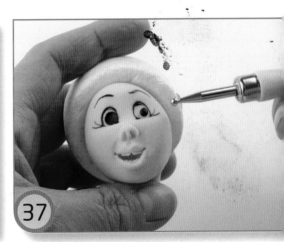

37 Add a black ball to the white of each eye and flatten using a small ball tool. Using small circular movements, stretch and position the black paste, leaving some of the surrounding white paste visible.

38 Mix a little white paste with a few drops of alcohol. Use a tiny brush to add a dot of white to each eye. The head is complete and ready to attach to the model.

17

CREATING EXPRESSIONS

Although all heads start in the same way, with the same basic features, it is easy to adapt them to personalise your figures. Gender and age can be determined with a slight variation in paintwork, while manipulating the mouth, when the paste is still soft, can make a huge difference to the facial expression. Here are a few examples to inspire you...

Gender can be determined easily in your paintwork: create thick eyebrows and only tiny eyelashes for a male face; create finer eyebrows and longer lashes for a female.

Leaving a little more white showing around the blacks of the eyes, and using raised eyebrows and an open mouth, can create an expression of shock or surprise.

Create chubby cheeks to make a model look younger, and use less paintwork on the eyes and eyebrows. An open mouth and gappy teeth can also add to the effect.

Add eyelids to give a more laid-back look to your figure. Manipulating the lower lip with the small ball tool, so that the figure is biting his lip, creates an expression of curiosity.

SKIN TONES

There are many skin tone paste colourings available, but I choose to blend colours together, as it allows for more variety of tone. I also feel it adds a little more warmth to the model. This is all a matter of personal taste so finding the right look for you is all about trying different options. To create any skin tone, I will colour white paste with autumn leaf and claret to create a caucasian tone, then darken gradually with brown as necessary.

You can easily create a gorgeous range of skin tones using white paste and a combination of just three paste colourings.

BLENDING SKIN TONES

Begin by adding autumn leaf gradually to a ball of white paste using the tip of a cocktail stick. This will create a golden brown that is too light for skin tone on its own. Dip the tip of a cocktail stick into claret paste colouring and dot the coloured paste three or four times. This seems a tiny amount, but the paste colouring is so concentrated that only the smallest addition is enough to add a little rosiness to the blend. This will give you a caucasian skin tone. To create a darker skin colour, gradually add dark brown to the mix and blend. Check the colour between blends to determine the darkness of the skin tone you want to achieve. Remember though, that the paste will dry darker than it looks at the kneading stage.

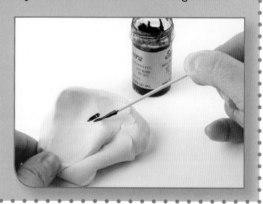

MAKING HANDS

Hands are very delicate to work into shape as the paste is so small – the key is not to flatten the paste paper thin. Keep a good enough thickness to be able to grasp each finger without crushing and breaking it. A light touch is required for this part of the model, as each finger is elongated individually. It takes patience and confidence, both of which will come more easily with practice.

Roll a pea-sized amount of paste into a ball. Form this into a teardrop shape and then flatten with your finger. Pinch around the wrist to make a stalk. Keeping the knife in line with the hand, cut almost half way down onto the hand to create the thumb and pull out to the side. Make three shorter cuts along the top of the hand to form the fingers.

Starting with the little finger, take the tip gently between your finger and thumb and roll and pull gently to lengthen. Repeat for each finger – the thumb will now be in proportion. Pinch around the thumb to smooth and soften the cut edge.

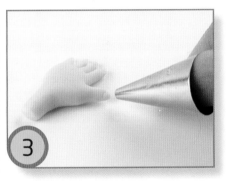

Use a small piping tip to make nail markings.

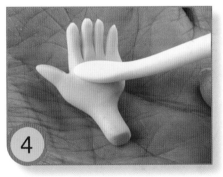

To add some movement, place the hand palm upwards on your hand. Using the rounded end of the leaf veiner, push onto the hand just below the finger cuts and pull swiftly forward as if wiping it clean. The fingers will curl slightly, just enough to enable you to move as required.

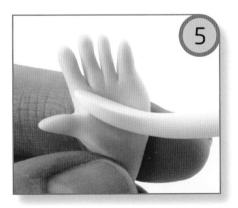

Push the rounded end of the veiner into the palm of the hand next to the thumb to pull it forward slightly.

With a final twist of the wrist to define the shape of the palm, the hand is complete.

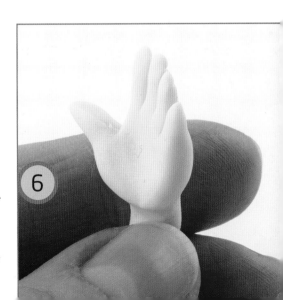

MAKING BARE ARMS

The size and thickness of the arms need to be in proportion to your model. Generally, the arm should be long enough that the hand rests at about mid-thigh height, but it is always best to roll a sausage of paste and judge it against the body of your model before you start, and then measure again once the arm is made – you can always adjust the arm if you feel it doesn't look quite right. The weights of paste that I used for every model are given with each project.

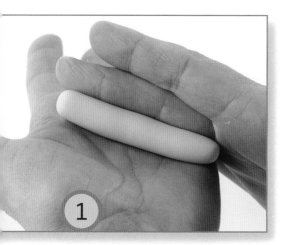

Roll the paste into a sausage using the length of your fingers to ensure an even roll. Roll until you reach a size and thickness that is roughly proportional to your model.

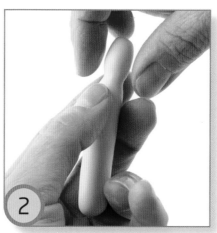

Pinch and twist one end of the sausage between each forefinger and thumb, to form the wrist.

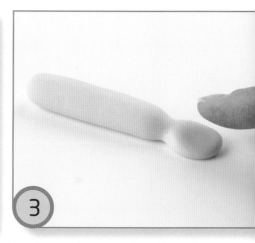

Lay the arm down on a clean, flat surface and flatten the hand.

Pinch the tip of the hand in slightly to form the shape of the fingers.

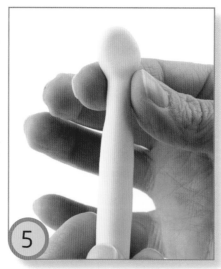

Hold the wrist between your finger and thumb and twist and pull the base of the arm gently, lengthening it slightly and tapering the wrist at the same time.

Keeping the knife in line with the arm, cut almost half way down onto the hand to create the thumb and pull it gently out to the side. Make three further shorter cuts along the top of the hand to form each finger.

20

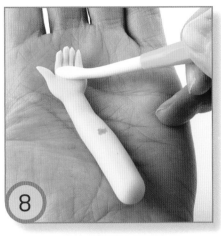

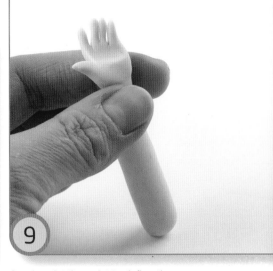

7 Gently roll and pull the fingers and thumb to lengthen them, and create nails using a piping tip – refer to steps 2 and 3 on page 19.

8 Shape the palm of the hand using the round end of the leaf veiner – refer to steps 4 and 5 on page 19.

9 Gently twist the wrist to define the hand shape.

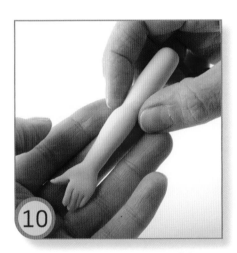

10 Pinch around the middle section of the arm to determine the elbow.

11 Roll the upper part of the arm between your finger and thumb. The top of the arm should be slightly thinner in appearance. The arm remains thicker near the elbow, tapering down to the wrist.

12 Pinch the elbow between your finger and thumb.

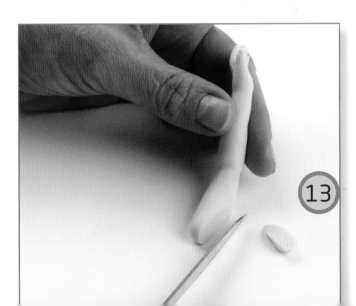

13 Cut the top of the shoulder at an angle before gluing into position.

MAKING BARE LEGS

As with the arms, the legs need to be in proportion to your model. Generally, my guide is that an adult leg should be twice the length of the body. However, when creating babies and small children you may want to make the legs slightly shorter. Use this rule as a guide, but trust your own judgement in the end.

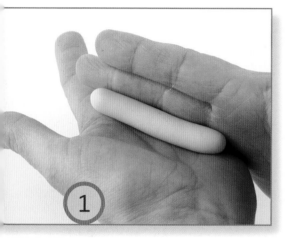

To make legs and feet, roll the paste into a sausage. Use the length of your finger to roll the paste evenly.

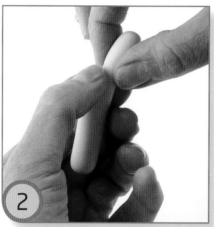

Pinch and twist at the ankle between each forefinger and thumb.

Flatten the front of the foot a little and bend forwards. Pinch around the heel to shape and smooth.

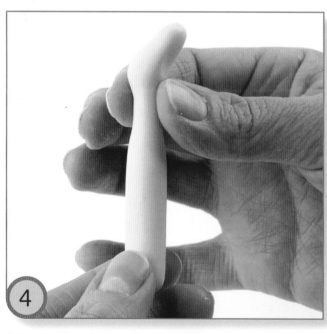

Roll the ankle and pull gently to lengthen and shape.

Flatten the front of the foot to lengthen.

Cut a diagonal line across the toes. The direction of the cut determines whether it is the right or left foot.

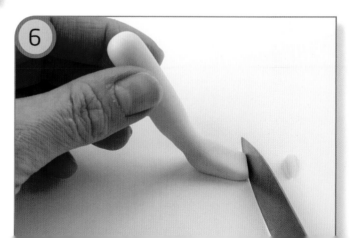

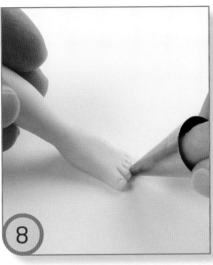

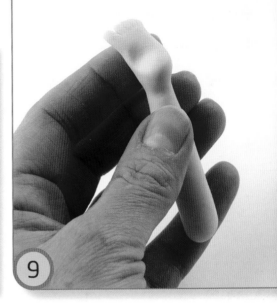

7 Make four small cuts into the foot, across the top of the diagonal edge, to form the toes. Make the first a little wider than the rest, for the big toe.

8 Make nail markings using the small end of a piping tip.

9 Indent the centre back of the foot with a finger to shape the instep.

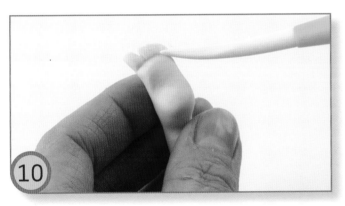

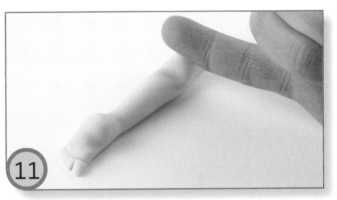

10 Push the sharp end of the leaf veiner into and under the back of the toes.

11 Indent the back of the knee with your finger.

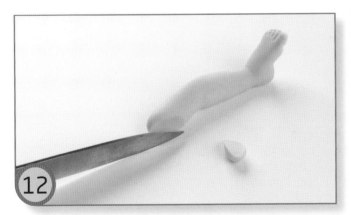

12 Bend the leg at the knee slightly, to suit the position of your model. Pinch the sides of the knee to reshape. Cut the inside top of the thigh at an angle to glue in position.

STORING YOUR FINISHED MODELS

Models should be stored in a cool, dry place and not in the refrigerator. The quick change in temperature will sweat the paste and leave unwanted markings on the paste when it dries. Some fondant (sugarpaste) will state on the packaging that it is good for storing in a refrigerator, but bear in mind that any part of the figure that has been painted or dusted will be affected differently.

I recommend that you store the models in a cool, dry place, away from direct light and humidity. I don't make models any sooner than two weeks ahead of time. The models will keep indefinitely depending on how you store them, but colours may fade over time.

Baby Shower

This cute baby topper will transform your cake into an adorable masterpiece, and make any baby shower that extra bit special. The figure is very simple to create, and can easily be made for a baby boy, or with other additional accessories. The key thing to remember when making the baby is to ensure that you colour up enough flesh-toned paste for her entire body at the beginning, as it can be very difficult to recreate exact skin tones, and it will be easy to spot if the shades don't quite match.

YOU WILL NEED

- 110g (3¾oz) modelling paste
- 5g (⅙oz) fondant (sugarpaste)
- Pea-sized amount black fondant (sugarpaste)
- Autumn leaf, claret, dark brown and chestnut colouring pastes
- Sugar glue (see page 8)
- Rose and white dusting powders
- Icing (powdered) sugar
- Corn flour (corn starch) for dusting
- Pure food-grade alcohol
- Small rolling pin
- Leaf veiner
- Small scissors
- Paintbrushes
- Dusting brush
- Small ball tool
- No.2 piping tip
- Sharp knife
- Snippers
- Cocktail sticks
- Small pieces of sponge for support
- Blossom cutters (optional)

Colour 90g (3⅕oz) of modelling paste to create the flesh tone you want (see page 18). You will use 35g (1¼oz) to make the body; store the remainder in a plastic bag until you are ready to use it. Roll your modelling paste into a cone shape. Create the baby's bottom by rolling your fingers across the centre of the cone to indent it, keeping the larger end of the cone rounded.

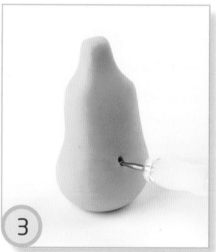

Make a neck by pinching around the top of the cone. Extend the neck gently with little pinching movements around the paste to narrow and lengthen it, creating shoulders as you do so. Smooth around the neck and shoulder area with your fingers.

Make a little tummy button with a small ball tool.

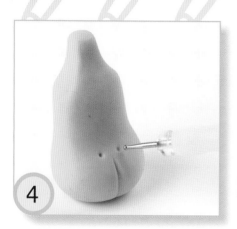

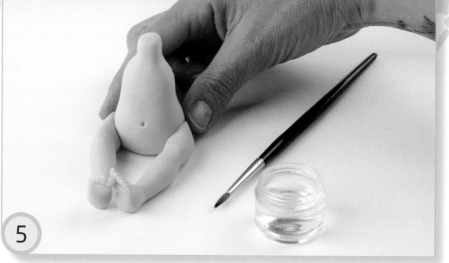

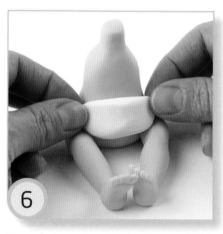

4

Use the sharp end of the leaf veiner to define the baby's bottom. Use a small ball tool to create two dimples in the lower back.

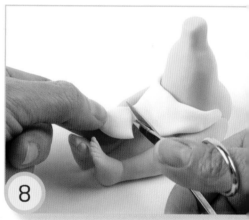

5

To make the legs, use 10g (²/₅oz) of flesh-coloured modelling paste for each leg and follow the instructions on pages 22–23. Trim off the top of each leg so that it sits well against the body, then glue into position with sugar glue as shown.

6

To make the nappy, use 7g (¼oz) of white modelling paste. Use half the amount to create the front piece. Pinch and stretch the paste across the front of the body to gauge the size.

7

Shape the nappy with your fingers to fit around the sides of the body and down between the legs.

8

Glue the front of the nappy into position, trimming away any excess with small scissors.

TOP TIP

A dry, flat dusting brush is ideal to neaten and smooth the smallest areas, where it is impossible to reach with a finger.

Tuck the front of the nappy neatly under the front of the body using a clean dusting brush. Then, pull the front of the nappy forward a little to show the tummy button.

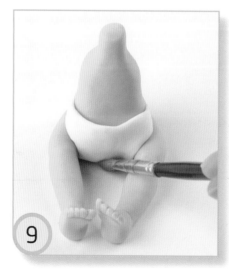

9

10

Repeat steps 6 and 7 to shape the back of the nappy using the remaining paste. Glue it into position, allowing the back sides to overlap the front sides slightly.

11

Trim away any excess modelling paste and tuck the bottom of the nappy neatly under the baby's bottom using a dusting brush.

12

Pull the back of the nappy outwards a little – use your thumb to support the base of the nappy.

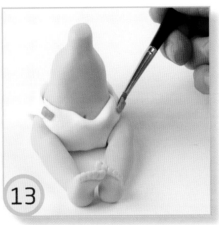

13

Colour 8g (¹⁄₃oz) of modelling paste with claret colouring. Use a tiny amount to make two little strips to attach on each side of the nappy, and set the remainder aside.

14

Push a cocktail stick at least two-thirds of the way down into the body through the neck. Trim the excess to leave approximately 1cm (½in) protruding.

To make the arms, use 8g (¹⁄₃oz) of flesh-coloured paste for each and follow the instructions on pages 20–21. Glue them into position. Use a small piece of sponge to support the arm that will later rest on a blanket. See page 30 for guidance on how to create the blanket.

15

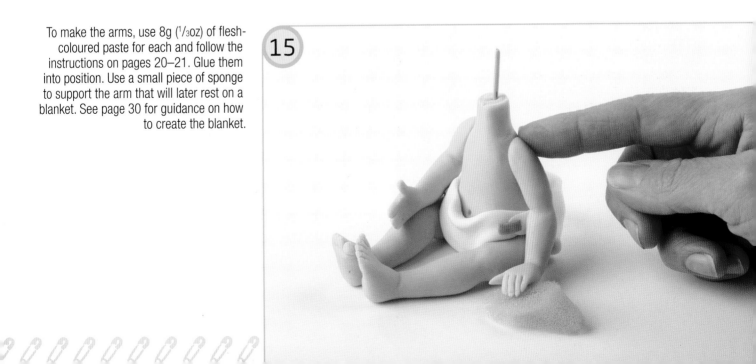

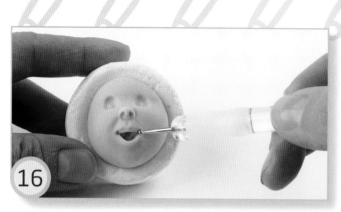

To make and shape the head, use 16g (²/₃oz) of flesh-coloured paste and follow the instructions on pages 12–17. As the baby's neck is formed as part of the body, follow the steps from 1–3 and then from 7 up to and including step 32.

Mix a little dark brown paste colouring with a few drops of alcohol until a smooth consistency is reached. Using the smallest paintbrush, paint the detail across the top of the eye as shown. Paint two tiny strokes for the eyebrows. Follow steps 36–38 on page 17 to finish.

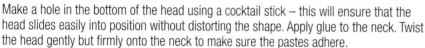

TOP TIP

Before gluing in position, place the head onto the body and check that the neck doesn't look too long. Remove the head and trim the neck to size if necessary.

Make a hole in the bottom of the head using a cocktail stick – this will ensure that the head slides easily into position without distorting the shape. Apply glue to the neck. Twist the head gently but firmly onto the neck to make sure the pastes adhere.

To make the ears, roll two tiny balls of flesh-coloured paste. Push a paintbrush handle into each ball. Apply glue to the sides of the head then transfer the indented balls onto the sides of the head. Push in the centre of each ear using the paintbrush handle and push slightly backwards. Leave the model to dry overnight before adding hair.

To create a hairstyle, colour 5g (¹/₆oz) of fondant (sugarpaste) with chestnut colouring. Use three-quarters of the paste and pinch to shape and fit around the head.

Carefully pull and stretch the hair to the required length, shaping the edges with your fingers.

Remove the paste to add texture before reapplying. With the sharp end of the leaf veiner, push down onto the hair using short, sharp rocking movements to score random lines. Follow the direction of the hair to create texture.

Apply glue to the crown of the head and around the base of the neck. Position the hair and tweak the lower edge with your fingers. Trim away any unwanted excess using small scissors to create style.

Use the remaining chestnut-coloured paste to roll varying lengths of teardrop shape – these will form the loose strands of hair around the baby's face. Apply glue to the base of the teardrop to secure it, then fold it carefully down around the face and secure with glue.

Use tools such as a leaf veiner or dry paintbrush to help with styling the smallest strands of hair – bend the ends of the teardrops up to form soft curls or waves.

Build up the hair by adding smaller teardrop shapes. Create little fly-away hairs by gluing strands in an upward position then pushing them forward with a leaf veiner. There is no need to add glue to the ends of these strands.

Use a tiny piece of claret paste to make a little bow. Roll two teardrop shapes, indent the centres using a leaf veiner, then fix in position with glue.

TIPS AND FINISHING TOUCHES

Use the remaining claret-coloured paste to make a blanket. Roll out the paste fairly thinly and cut a rectangle. Emboss the rectangle with blossom cutters to create a pattern. You can also use embossing rolling pins for this – the design is entirely up to you. Fold and twist the rectangle into a loosely scrunched blanket shape and slide it underneath the supported hand to finish.

You can apply additional layers of paste to the hair for extra fullness, if you wish. Glue the extra hair in place – the overlapping pastes can then be textured to blend any seams together.

A bow is a cute finishing touch and very simple to make. Only secure it once you are happy with the arrangement of the hair.

Instead of positioning the limbs of the model so that they stick out in a straight line, play around with the feet once the legs are glued in position but are still fairly pliable. A little twist of the ankles can make all the difference to the charm and character of your model. Apply a little glue where the pastes meet to secure.

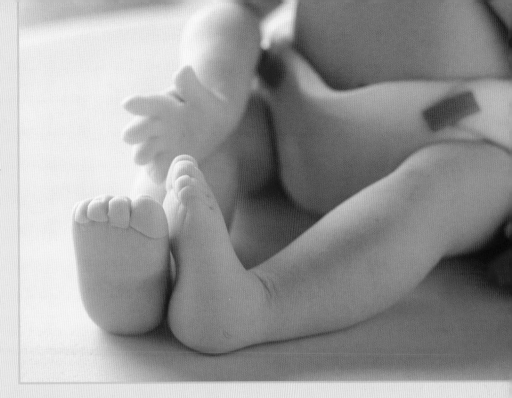

Why not personalise the model to suit your occasion? With a different hairstyle, this model could easily be created as a boy. If you do want to create a boy, the paintwork around the eyes should be much the same but with slightly shorter eyelashes. Use a few shorter wisps of hair at the front, and stroke down the hair at the back of the neck using a clean, flat dusting brush.

31

First Birthday

This happy little chappy is having a great time on his birthday! As with all the projects in the book, you could easily adapt the instructions given to make the figure look more like the child you know, and you could easily substitute the number 1 candle for presents, toys or simply use a real candle in its place.

YOU WILL NEED

- 175g (6¹/₆oz) modelling paste
- 10g (²/₅oz) fondant (sugarpaste)
- 20g (¾oz) gum paste (flower paste)
- Sugar glue (see page 8)
- Autumn leaf, claret, peach, Christmas red, party green, ice blue, caramel/ivory, chestnut, dark brown and yellow colouring pastes
- Rose, white, orange and gold lustre dust colours
- Icing (powdered) sugar
- Corn flour (corn starch) for dusting
- Pure food-grade alcohol
- Small rolling pin
- Leaf veiner
- Bone tool
- Small stitching wheel
- Paintbrushes
- Dusting brush
- Small ball tool
- No.1 and no.2 piping tips
- Sharp knife
- Snippers
- Cocktail sticks
- Small pieces of sponge for support

To make the trousers, colour 90g (3¹/₅oz) of modelling paste with party green colouring. Roll the paste into a sausage. Leave approximately 2.5cm (1in) of thickness in the centre and roll either side to lengthen each leg equally.

Fold the sausage in half, bringing the legs almost together, as shown.

Pinch a small amount of the paste upwards in the centre – this will help to support the jacket later.

4

Trim the ends of the legs so that they are the same length, then flatten around the bottom of each trouser leg. Pinch around the edge to sharpen.

5

Indent the back of each leg, behind each knee, using a finger. Pinch the sides of the knees to reshape them before bending the legs slightly, into a relaxed position.

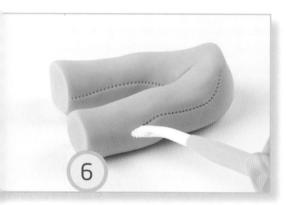

6

Add some detail to the inner and outer lengths of the legs using a small stitching wheel.

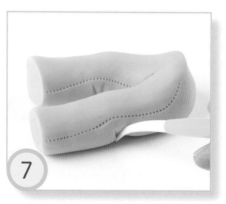

7

Create creases under each knee using the sharp end of the leaf veiner.

8

Use 7g (¼oz) of white paste to make each shoe. Roll into a cone shape and flatten slightly. Pinch around the bottom of the shoe to sharpen the sole. Pinch the heel in at the sides to narrow.

9

Colour a small amount of paste caramel/ivory – enough to make two pea-sized balls. Roll one ball into a sausage that fits the length of the shoe from toe to heel.

10

Shape the paste to fit the sole of the shoe by pinching, stretching and flattening it with your fingers.

Glue into position on the sole of the shoe and smooth around the seam with your fingers to blend.

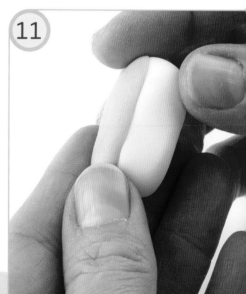

11

Mark the sole of the shoe using a knife. Use the blunt side of the blade to create a deep indent at the heel. Use the sharp side of the knife to create some shallower, parallel lines on the top half of the sole. Pinch again at the sides of the heel to reshape.

Repeat steps 9–12 to create the other shoe. Using a small amount of sugar glue, attach both shoes to the trouser bottoms.

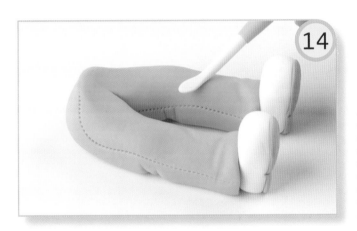

Add a little more detail to the trousers by gently pushing the rounded end of the leaf veiner into the paste to create wide creases and folds at the knees and ankles.

TOP TIP

As a rough guide to proportion, the length of the body should equal the length from thigh to knee or knee to ankle on the model.

To make the jacket and sleeves, colour 55g (2oz) of paste Christmas red with a touch of peach. This blend of colour will create a deep orange shade. To make the torso, use 35g (1¼oz) and set the remainder aside. Roll the paste into a cone shape using your palms, and flatten slightly.

Pinch around the wider, bottom edge gradually to shape and widen. Make a hollow in the centre with your finger – the red paste will then sit neatly and securely on top of the raised area of paste you created in step 3.

Apply a small amount of sugar glue to the hollowed paste.

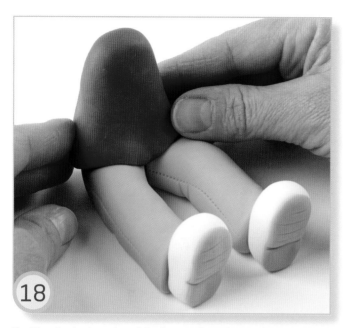

Position the body on top of the legs and gently stretch and smooth the paste downwards slightly so that the bottom of the jacket overlaps the thighs a little.

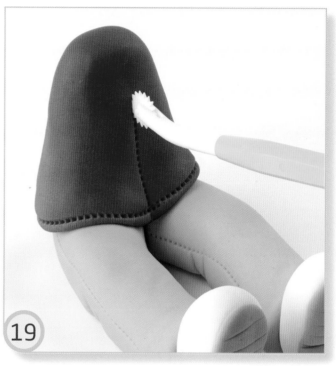

Add detail around the bottom edge and centre of the jacket using the small stitching wheel.

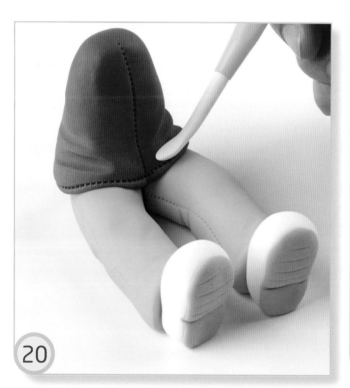

Create folds and creases on each side of the body using the rounded end of the leaf veiner. Try to imitate the natural folds of a garment.

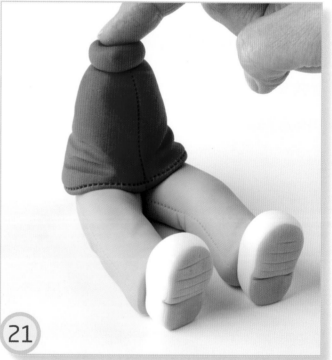

Roll a pea-sized amount of red-orange paste into a ball and glue it onto the neck of the jacket. Flatten it with your finger to create an indent in the centre.

Using small, circular movements with a large ball tool, smooth around the inside of the neck indent to hollow and widen.

Add the final detail to the neck using the small stitching wheel, as shown. Insert a cocktail stick at least two-thirds of the way into the body through the neck. Trim the excess using snippers, leaving approximately 1cm (½in) protruding. Leave the body to dry overnight.

Colour 16g (²/₃oz) of modelling paste with flesh tones, see page 18. Take off 14g (½oz) to make the head and set the remainder aside for the hands. To make a head with simple detail, roll the paste into a cone shape and flatten slightly.

Indent across the front of the thinner end of the cone with your finger, to form the eye area. Keeping the face more pear-shaped than oval, pinch the chin just a little.

Support the head in polystyrene mould. Create a hole in the centre of the face using a small ball tool. Make a tiny teardrop shape for the nose and glue in position in the hole, flattening slightly.

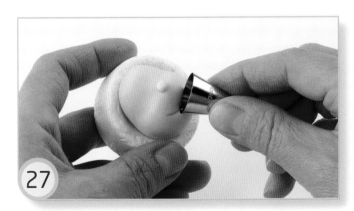

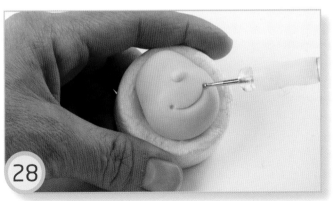

Use the bottom end of a piping tip to create a smile. Push into the centre of the face and roll upwards to the left and right to complete the curve.

Add a dimple at either side of the smile, using a small ball tool.

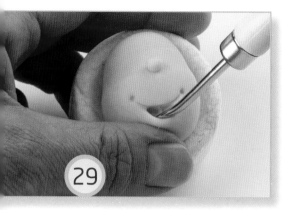

29

Open the mouth a little using the wide end of a metal leaf veiner. Place onto the centre of the mouth with the rounded end facing downwards and pull the paste down gently. Using your thumb to support underneath the lip, move the veiner back and forth along the inside of the mouth to shape and smooth. Move your supporting thumb along the mouth as you work each little section. Pull the top of the lip outwards slightly.

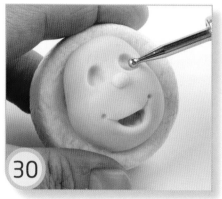

30

Hollow the eye sockets, using a small ball tool to shape as shown.

31

Fill the hollows with two tiny balls of flesh-coloured paste, to make eyelids. The eyelids should appear slightly rounded and should not be flat against the face.

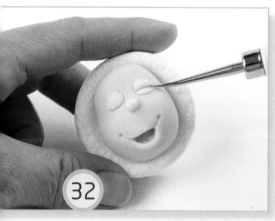

32

Using the sharp end of a metal leaf veiner, gently indent across each eye. Begin from the inside corner of the eye and work towards the outside corner at a slight angle.

33

Sweep the top lid gently downward using light strokes with the wide end of the leaf veiner to close the gap just a little.

34

Mix dark brown paste colour with a few drops of alcohol. Using a fine paintbrush, carefully paint along the eye line as shown. Paint two small lines for eyebrows. Follow the instructions on page 16 to colour the cheeks and add teeth.

35

To avoid distorting the head before fixing in place, push a cocktail stick up into the head through the neck area to make a hole. Glue around the neck of the jacket and place the head in position, twisting as it meets the neck to ensure the pastes have adhered.

36 Roll two tiny flesh-coloured balls for the ears. Hold the balls against the side of the head to gauge the proportion.

37 Push the paintbrush handle into each ball. Apply glue to the sides of the head and attach the ears, releasing the paintbrush.

38 Indent the centre of the ears with the paintbrush handle and push them back slightly.

39 To create a hairstyle, colour 10g (²/₅oz) of fondant (sugarpaste) with chestnut colouring. Roll into a ball.

40 Pinch and stretch the paste so that it fits across the top of the head from ear to ear. Using the head as a guide, begin to pinch and stretch the bottom of the paste to almost fit the back of the head. Remove the hair.

TOP TIP

I recommend using fondant (sugarpaste) for the hair as the paste will blend and move easily into position around the head. Modelling paste will be too heavy and less pliable.

Apply glue to the top and back of the head. Replace the paste on the head and begin to shape using the tips of your fingers, gently pulling the paste to the areas you want it to cover. The heat from your fingers on the fondant (sugarpaste) will enable the paste to blend easily onto the head. Use small strokes and take your time.

41

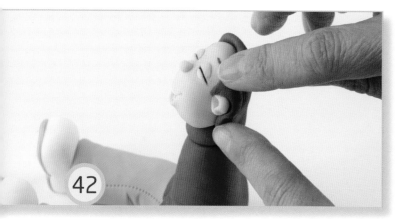

42 Work the paste carefully around the ears, smoothing it with your fingertips.

43 Pinch along the top of the hairline randomly to create raised spikes of hair.

44 Mix gold dust powder with a few drops of alcohol to create a paintable consistency. Using a fine paintbrush, paint along the zip line on the front of the jacket.

45 Make a tiny fastener for the top of the jacket. Cut a circle using the no.2 piping tip and flatten. Cut the inside out with the no.1 piping tip and carefully flick the paste ring off the tip. Apply glue to the top of the jacket and use a damp paintbrush to lift the ring into position. Paint with gold (see page 42 for further guidance).

46 Use two pea-sized amounts of flesh-coloured paste to make hands, following the instructions on page 19. To make the sleeves, use 8g ($^1/_3$oz) of red-orange paste for each. Roll a sausage shape, using the length of your fingers to keep the paste smooth.

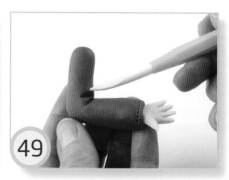

47 Indent the centre of the sleeve then bend it to 90-degrees to create a bent arm. Pinch at the sides of the elbow to reshape. Flatten the cuff end with your finger then pinch around the edges to sharpen.

48 Make a hollow inside the cuff to make room for the hand. Push the handle of a paintbrush into the cuff and rotate to widen. Apply sugar glue inside the hollow, right down to the inside edge of the cuff.

49 Place the hand in position and smooth the cuff down around it. Make creases at the elbow using the sharp end of the leaf veiner. Add detail around the cuff using the small stitching wheel.

40

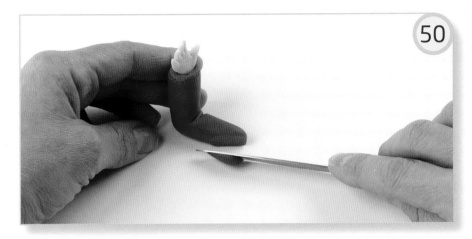

Cut the top inside of the shoulder at an angle. This will create a less bulky arm when positioned on your model.

51

52

53

Apply glue to the trimmed end of the arm and position on the body. Use a small piece of sponge to support the arm in place, as shown.

Make the other arm following steps 46–49, but don't fully bend it. Cut straight down across the top of the arm, as shown.

Use a cocktail stick to make a hole in the shoulder area of the body, at the angle the arm will be placed.

54

Carefully push the cocktail stick half way into the arm through the shoulder end. Leave approximately 1cm (½in) protruding. Cut any excess using snippers. Apply glue around the flattened shoulder area of the arm and slide the arm into position. Use the tips of your fingers to gently smooth the seams. Use a dry dusting brush to help you if necessary.

Support the raised arm of the model with a piece of sponge, and leave to dry overnight.

55

TIPS AND FINISHING TOUCHES

Glue the model into position on your cake and complete the design by adding a number candle. You could use a real candle if you wish or you can make your own edible version. To make the candle, colour 20g (¾oz) of gum paste (flower paste) blue. Roll to approximately 5mm (¼in) thick and use the template on page 128 as a guide. Cut a few circles of white paste to decorate and use a small ball tool to make a small hole in the top of the number. Colour a pea-sized amount of gum paste (flower paste) yellow. Roll into a teardrop shape, leaving a small 'plug' of paste at the bottom, and flatten. Shape the tip of the teardrop to a flame-like point. Apply a small amount of glue to the hole on the top of your shape, then insert the 'plug' of the flame to secure it. Dust around the base of the flame using orange dust powder for effect. Leave to dry flat overnight.

Gold powder dusts are available from craft stores. They are extremely fine and very little is needed to add the finishing touches to details such as zips. I add a couple of drops of alcohol into a pot and dip a paintbrush into this to dampen the bristles. Dip the damp brush into the gold powder and then return it to the alcohol in the mixing pot to blend. This will prevent the powder flying into the air and settling on everything around! Paint the detail onto the jacket using a fine paintbrush.

42

An open hand on the model leaves room for more detail to be added later. You could make a little cupcake and place it on the hand, or even a birthday card – anything you like to personalise the model to your own taste. Your model's eyes could also be open (see pages 16–17), although I do like this giggly expression!

If you wanted, you could also add a little more detail to the shoes. Edible pens can be used for decorating and it would be easy to add a few spots or lines to make a pattern. Use the pens on paste that is completely dry. This will help if you if you have a tendency to be heavy handed. Paste colour mixed with alcohol and painted on is another option.

A change of hairstyle and colour is all you need to create a female model. Adding more detail to the trousers using a different colour paste and cutting out small blossoms using cutters will give them the feminine touch – be adventurous.

43

Engagement

What better way to commemorate that special moment than by recreating it in sugar? Make these toppers as personal to the happy couple as you can – try to incorporate their hairstyles and favourite outfits, and don't forget to make the ring the centre of attention by adding silver and gold lustre to it to make it sparkle!

YOU WILL NEED

- 90g (3¹/₅oz) black fondant (sugarpaste)
- 215g (7²/₃oz) modelling paste
- 15g (½oz) fondant (sugarpaste)
- Autumn leaf, claret, dark brown, chestnut, ruby, ice blue and navy colouring pastes
- Sugar glue (see page 8)
- CMC (tylose) powder
- Rose, white, gold and silver dusting powders
- Small rolling pin
- Corn flour (corn starch)
- Leaf veiner
- Small scissors
- Paintbrushes
- Small ball tool
- Medium ball tool
- Cutting wheel
- Stitching wheel
- No.4 and no.7 piping tips
- Sharp knife
- Snippers
- Cocktail sticks
- Kebab skewers
- Small pieces of sponge for support
- Pure food-grade alcohol
- Blossom cutters

Make 90g (3¹/₅oz) of modelling paste using ready-made black fondant (sugarpaste) – sprinkle just under ¼ tsp CMC (tylose) powder onto your work surface and knead into the paste until incorporated. Use 75g (2²/₃oz) to make the trousers and set aside the rest. Roll the paste into a sausage. Leave the centre point slightly thick and roll from either side to lengthen each leg.

To get the proportion required, roll each leg individually by rolling and gently pulling from the centre of each leg towards the end of the trouser.

Pinch around the bottom of each trouser leg to sharpen and shape.

44

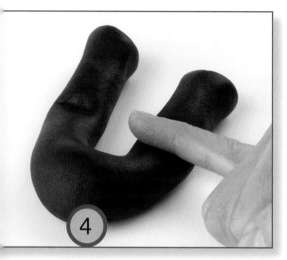

To make it easier to bend the leg without cracking the paste, indent behind each knee with a finger.

Bend each leg – place one thumb on top of the thigh and the other just below the knee. Pinch the knee with your thumbs, without allowing your thumbs to meet. The aim is to sharpen the knee a little, and take away the roundness, without making a determined crease.

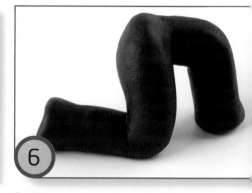

Position the legs as shown, bringing one knee forwards.

Add some creases to the backs of the knees and the bottom of each leg using the wide end of a leaf veiner. Leave to dry overnight.

To make the shoes, use 4g (1/6oz) of black modelling paste for each. Roll into a sausage, tapering the shape slightly at one end to form the heel.

Pinch around the edge of the sole to sharpen.

Use the sharp side of the knife to mark around the bottom edge of the shoe. Start from the heel and work your way around leaving a fine line.

Indent the heel using the blunt side of the knife.

Pinch either side of the heel to shape.

13

Apply a small amount of sugar glue to the top of each shoe and position at the base of each trouser leg.

14

Indent the shoe on the right leg slightly with your finger to give it some movement.

15

Support the legs with sponge and leave to dry completely.

16

To make the shirt, colour 46g (1²/₃oz) of modelling paste ice blue. Use 30g (1oz) for the torso and set the remainder aside. Roll into a cone shape and flatten slightly.

17

Pinch around the bottom of the cone to widen and shape. Make a hollow in the centre with your fingers.

18

Add detail to the front of the shirt by running a cutting wheel from the bottom up to the neck.

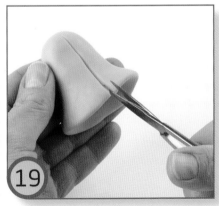

19

Use small, sharp scissors to snip a little way into the bottom of the shirt, along the line you just created, to open it slightly. Pinch either side of the cut to neaten and shape.

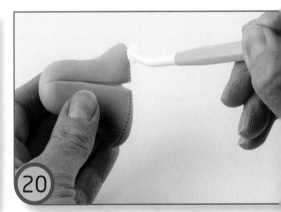

20

Use a stitching wheel to add detail all the way around the bottom edge of the shirt.

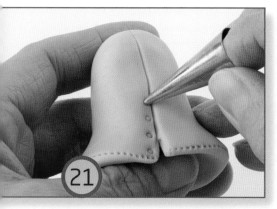

21

Place a small piping tip on the end of your finger and indent several times up the left-hand side of your central line to indicate buttons.

22

Using sugar glue, secure the torso on top of the legs, smoothing the bottom edges down and around the top of the trousers. Use the wide, rounded end of the leaf veiner to create creases in the sides and around the bottom edge.

23

Work a medium ball tool into the neck area using small circular movements to widen and hollow.

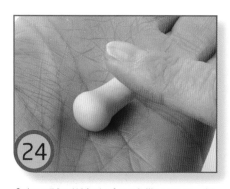

24

Colour 50g (1¾oz) of modelling paste with flesh tones, see page 18. Use a pea-sized amount to make the neck and set the remainder aside. To make the neck, roll a bean shape. With a finger, roll in the centre and out towards one end to lengthen, keeping the other end rounded.

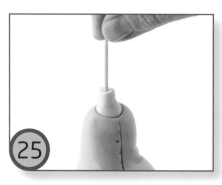

25

Glue the neck into position in the hollow of the shirt, smoothing the rounded end down to fit. Trim the neck to size. Push a cocktail stick into the neck and halfway down into the body. Trim away the excess, leaving at least 1cm (½in) protruding.

26

To make the collar, roll a pea-sized amount of white paste and cut into a small rectangle. Cut across the rectangle diagonally to make two triangles. Arrange the triangles on your work surface with the straight edges facing each other to resemble boat sails.

27

Apply glue around the neck of the shirt. Position the collar, attaching the straight edge of each piece around the neck as shown.

Make the hands following the instructions on page 19, using a pea-sized amount of flesh-coloured paste for each one. Set aside while you make the sleeves. Use 8g (1/3oz) of ice blue paste for each sleeve, and follow the instructions on pages 40–41. Glue into position and support with sponge.

28

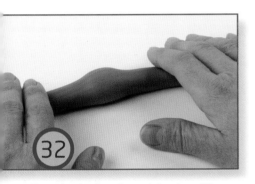

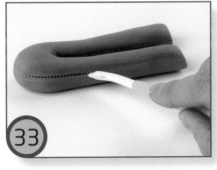

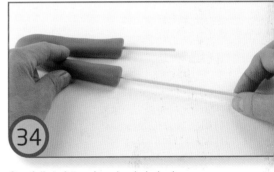

29 To make the head, use 15g (½oz) of flesh-coloured paste and follow steps 24–30 on pages 37–38. To create the eyeballs, follow the instructions on pages 16–17. Paint smaller lashes on the outside corner of each eye and thicken the brow slightly to determine the male character. Create a guiding hole in the bottom of the head with a cocktail stick, then glue the head in position and leave the model to dry overnight.

30 Colour 5g (⅙oz) of fondant (sugarpaste) with chestnut. Roll a ball and pinch it with your fingers to flatten. Use enough to cover the back of the crown and leave the remaining paste aside. Before applying glue to the head, fix and stretch the paste into position, allowing the heat of your fingers to pull the paste gently to fit along the neckline. Carefully remove the paste and texture with the sharp end of the leaf veiner. Push the veiner into the paste with short, sharp strokes following the hairline.

31 Apply glue to the head and attach the textured hair. Smooth the edges into position and adjust the texturing with the veiner if necessary. Roll several tiny teardrops using the remaining paste and attach to the front and sides of the hair to complete the style.

32 To make the female model, colour 60g (2¹/₁₀oz) of modelling paste navy blue. Roll into a sausage shape. Leave the centre slightly thick and roll either side to lengthen each leg.

33 Bend in the centre and bring the legs together. Flatten the bottom of each trouser leg with your finger. Add detail along the sides of the trousers using a stitching wheel.

34 Carefully twist and push a kebab skewer into each leg to reach the top of the thigh. Support the leg with one hand, to prevent any cracking in the paste. Trim any excess, leaving approximately 5cm (2in) of the skewer showing.

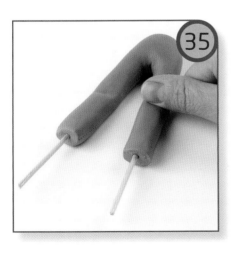

35 Indent the back of the knees slightly with your finger. Add a few creases underneath the bottom and on the trouser legs using the wide end of a leaf veiner for added detail.

To make a foot, use a pea-sized amount of flesh-coloured paste and roll into a teardrop shape. Pinch the rounded end to flatten and pull forwards.

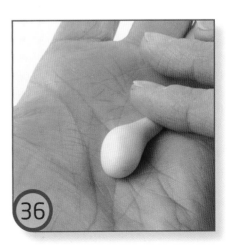

49

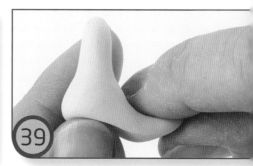

37 Pinch around the heel to smooth and shape, still keeping the heel rounded.

38 Flatten the front of the foot and pinch to lengthen.

39 Push the heel upwards and pull the toes down and outwards to create a curve in the bottom of the foot.

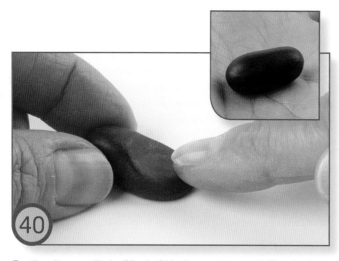

40 For the shoes, split 4g (¹⁄₆oz) of black paste in two. Roll each piece into a bean shape. Flatten the front, then pinch the sides and around the bottom edge to shape.

41 Glue each foot into position on top of a shoe. Roll a pea-sized amount of black paste and cut out two circles using the wide end of a piping tip.

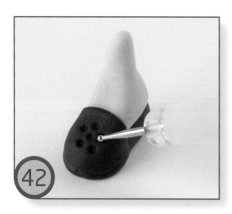

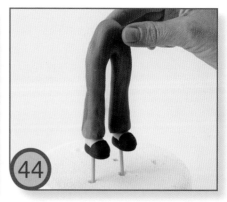

42 Pull each circle at either side to stretch it over the end of a shoe. Glue in position, covering the toes. Smooth the seams with your finger to make a neat join. Add a little detail using a small ball tool, if you want.

43 Before attaching the shoes to the trousers, use a kebab skewer to make a hole through the bottom of each shoe, up through the ankle. This will lessen the chance of distorting the shoes when they are skewered in place beneath the trouser legs.

44 Apply glue around the underside of each trouser leg and feed the shoes onto the supporting skewers to meet the trousers. Twist a little to make sure the pastes adhere. Use a polystyrene dummy cake to support the model as it stands and leave to dry overnight.

Use 45g (1²/₃oz) of white paste to make the woman's tunic. First, roll a thick sausage. Roll just underneath the bust line with your finger to indent, then move towards the bottom to lengthen a little and keep both ends rounded.

Pinch around the hemline of the tunic to thin the edge and widen to form a skirt.

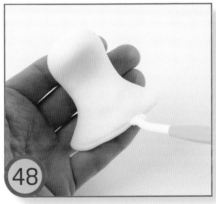

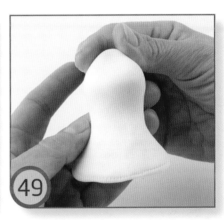

Pinch and stretch to the desired length, making a hollow in the centre with your fingers.

Add detail around the lower edge of the skirt with a stitching wheel.

Pinch the top of the tunic to form a rounded point – this is where you will create the neckline.

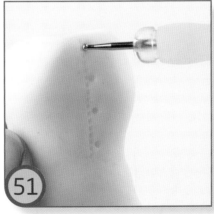

Use a medium ball tool to hollow out a space for the neck. Apply gentle pressure and use circular movements to gradually widen.

Add detail to the back of the tunic with a stitching wheel and a small ball tool, as shown.

To make the neck, use a pea-sized amount of flesh-coloured paste and roll a small, rounded sausage shape. Roll from the centre out towards one end to lengthen, keeping the other end rounded.

51

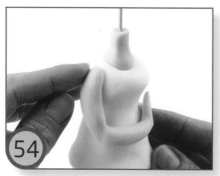

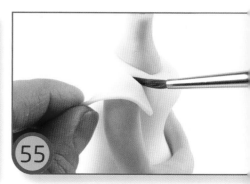

53 Glue into position with the rounded end fitting neatly into the hollow of the tunic. Trim the neck to size. Push a cocktail stick into the neck and halfway down into the body. Snip away the excess to leave at least 1cm (½in) protruding. Apply glue around the hollow of the skirt and position the tunic on the legs. Leave the model to dry overnight.

54 To make the right arm, use 6g (¹⁄₅oz) of flesh-coloured paste and follow the instructions on page 20. Apply glue to the inside of the shoulder and attach to the body, placing the hand around the waist and applying glue wherever the pastes meet.

55 Cut a circle of thin white paste using a piping tip. Cut across the circle, about three-quarters of the way down, to form a semi-circle with a straight edge. Stretch the straight edge wide enough to fit around the arm. Apply glue to the shoulder and place the rounded edge over the seam.

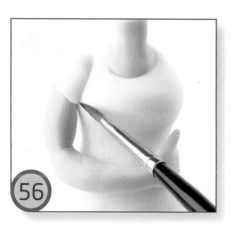

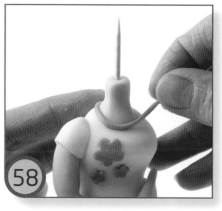

56 Use a damp paintbrush to tease the remaining half circle into place around the arm, to neaten and close the join.

57 For the trimmings on the tunic, colour a pea-sized amount of paste with a small amount of ruby or claret. Roll the paste and cut a few small blossoms using cutters. Attach the blossoms to the tunic where desired.

58 Roll a tiny sausage from the remaining pink paste to fit around the neck of the tunic, hiding the seam at the neckline.

To make the head, use 15g (½oz) of flesh-coloured paste and follow steps 24–30 on pages 37–38. To create the eyeballs, follow the instructions on pages 16–17. Paint long lashes on the outside corner of each eye and add a thin line for each eyebrow. Create a guiding hole in the bottom of the head with a cocktail stick, then glue the head in position and leave to dry for at least an hour before adding the hair.

TOP TIP

I recommend that you leave the model to dry overnight before adding the additional weight of a hairstyle. A freshly glued head may not withstand the pressure as you texture the hair.

Colour 8g (1/3oz) of fondant (sugarpaste) chestnut. Roll into a ball and flatten, pinching around the edges with your fingers to stretch and lengthen the paste to fit around the back of the crown, touching the shoulders. Use the sharp end of a leaf veiner to texture the shape, scoring the paste randomly with vertical marks. Snip the edges for added texture using small scissors.

Apply glue to the crown and attach the hair, gently pressing it into position without distorting the textured lines. Leave a gap around the shoulder on the side of the model where the remaining arm will be placed. The hair will still be pliable enough to rest on the arm once it is finally in position.

Roll several teardrops in varying sizes from the remaining paste. Attach these to the hair to create volume and style. Flick the ends outwards using a paintbrush.

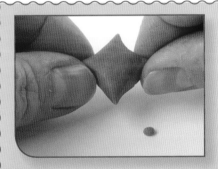

Make the second arm using 6g (1/5oz) of flesh-coloured paste, following the instructions on page 20. Apply glue to the inside of the shoulder and attach to the body. Apply a little glue to the inside of the hand so it is tacky to touch. Place it across the chin as shown. Hold in place for a few seconds to dry. Adjust the hair using a paintbrush; add a few more strands to complete the style.

To make a tiny cushion, colour a pea-sized amount of paste claret. Roll into a ball and flatten slightly. Pinch out four corners to make a square. Detail around the sides of the cushion with a stitching wheel and make several creases radiating out from the centre. Roll a tiny ball to form a button, place in the centre and flatten. For the engagement ring, use two sizes of small piping tips. Roll out some of the remaining flesh-coloured paste. Cut a circle with the larger of the two tips and flatten with your finger. Place the smaller tip in the centre and cut all the way through, leaving a tiny ring of paste around the end of the piping tip. Carefully remove this and pick up and place on the cushion using a damp glue brush. The tiny amount of glue from the brush should be enough to keep this in place. Roll and attach a tiny ball of paste for the diamond.

TIPS AND FINISHING TOUCHES

You can add a little more detail to the tunic by making a tiny bow from the remaining scraps of paste. Add a small strip to the back of the waist, attached on either side of the tunic. Cut two short strips, and cut the end of each at an angle. Glue these in position as hanging ribbons. Cut two short strips, fold each over to make a loop and glue in the centre. Cut away any excess to leave two loops. Attach at either side of the hanging ribbons and hide the seam with a small rectangle of paste. Neaten the edges, tucking them out of sight using the tip of a damp paintbrush.

Hair and make-up changes the personality of each model. I tried to create a 'rock chick' hairstyle here, but you never know quite how it's going to turn out until you start, and sometimes the style takes on a mind of its own. All in all it's part of the charm and creative flow. Just remember there is no right or wrong here. You can do whatever you like and personalise each model to make it your own.

The use of bold lustre powders mixed with alcohol can really highlight the smallest aspect of any project. The powder is very flyaway, making everything around you sparkle as it lands. I try to avoid this by dipping a fine paintbrush in alcohol and picking up the powder with the wet bristles. Mix your desired painting consistency and carefully touch the edges of the tiny ring to colour. Repeat using silver lustre powder for the stone.

54

If the head is left to dry completely, you will be able to texture the hair while it is in position. Otherwise, texture the hair first, then attach it. Whichever method comes easiest to you as the creator is the way to go. Have fun with it and be creative.

A happy boy indeed! If you want to create a bigger grin, pull the bottom lip down further and work the smile line a little wider.

With both models complete, it's time to secure them on top of the cake. I suggest using a little royal icing to attach these types of models – it is like edible cement. Any model you create that you feel has the potential to tip over in transit would benefit from it. The standing model has the added support of the skewers, but a spot of royal icing under each shoe, left to dry completely, elimates any worry.

55

Graduation

This proud little figure could easily be made as a female, and adapted to suit the colours of the school, college or university in question. Although this is a standing figure, and will need adequate support using kebab skewers, the gown helps to make it a little more sturdy. Remember to allow the figure's hair to dry completely before you add the cap, to ensure that it adheres securely without warping the paste underneath.

YOU WILL NEED

- 150g (5¹/₃oz) black fondant (sugarpaste)
- 60g (2¹/₁₀oz) modelling paste
- 5g (¹/₆oz) fondant (sugarpaste)
- Autumn leaf, claret, dark brown, chestnut and Christmas red colouring pastes
- Sugar glue (see page 8)
- Corn flour (corn starch)
- Rose and white dusting powders
- CMC (tylose) powder
- Small rolling pin
- Leaf veiner
- Small scissors
- Paintbrushes
- Small ball tool
- Medium ball tool
- Pure food-grade alcohol
- Thin strip cutter (optional)
- Sharp knife
- Snippers
- Cocktail sticks
- Kebab skewers

Make 150g (5¹/₃oz) of black modelling paste: follow the instructions on page 8, using ready-made black fondant (sugarpaste) and ¼ tsp of CMC (tylose) powder. Use 75g (2²/₃oz) to make the trousers and set aside the remainder in a plastic bag. Roll the paste into a sausage of the desired length and thickness.

Pinch around each end of the sausage to sharpen and shape the hem of each trouser leg.

Indent the centre of the sausage with your finger, then bend the sausage in half to bring the legs together in a standing position.

Make a pair of black shoes following steps 8–12 on page 46. Apply a small amount of glue to the top of each shoe, then push a kebab skewer through each shoe and up into each leg to about thigh level, carefully supporting each leg with one hand as you do so. Trim the excess to leave about 5cm (2in) of the skewer showing.

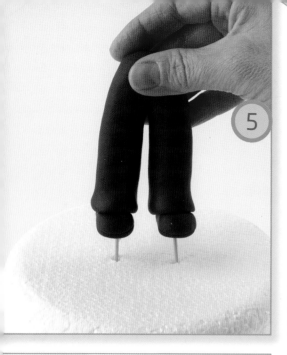

Use a polystyrene dummy to support the model as it stands.

5

TOP TIP

Using a polystyrene dummy to support standing models is ideal. Make holes in the dummy so that the skewer supports in the legs can be fed into them easily, and the complete model can be removed without pressure.

6

To make the torso, roll 35g (1¼oz) of white paste into a cone shape and flatten slightly. Pinch around the bottom edge to widen to fit neatly on top of the trousers. Glue into position. Leave the model to dry overnight.

7

For the cloak, roll 40g (1²/₅oz) of black modelling paste into a thin rectangle wide enough to wrap around the model. Trim and straighten the two long sides of the rectangle.

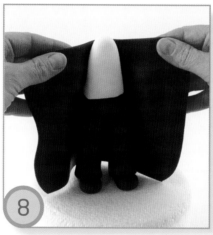

8

Hold the cloak against the back of the model, with a long, straight edge resting below the bottom of the trousers. Mark the cloak where it meets the top of the body using the tip of a knife. Lay the rectangle flat to trim across the top, cutting away any excess to create a straight edge. Apply glue to the back of the model, across the top and around the shoulder area.

9

Wrap the cloak around the model, pressing gently at the back and sides of the shoulders so that the cloak takes hold. Bring both sides of the cloak to the front and pinch together close to the body from the neck to halfway down. Trim with scissors from the top of the cloak and work downwards to cut away the excess. The cloak will fall open at the front at this point. Apply a little glue down the front of the torso and bring the sides of the cloak together again, pressing gently to secure them.

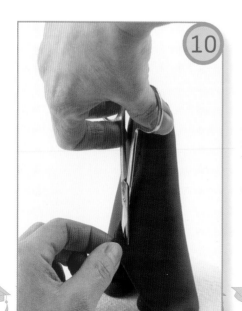

10

Decide at what point the cloak should fall open, and trim each side individually with scissors, working downwards at an angle to create an open cloak. Apply a little glue, if necessary, where the two sides of the cloak meet to secure them in place.

TOP TIP

Work carefully and slowly, snipping away a little bit at a time, to achieve a symmetrical shape.

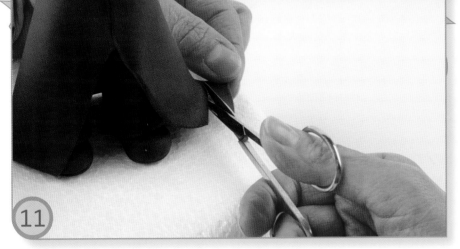

11 Shape the bottom of the cloak by trimming with scissors. Start from the open edge and work towards the back on each side, leaving a neat and even length.

12 Colour 20g (¾oz) of modelling paste with flesh tones. Make two hands following the instructions on page 19, leaving the remaining paste in a plastic bag. Set the hands aside while you make the sleeves.

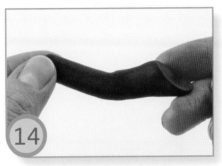

13 Use 10g (²/₅oz) of black paste for each sleeve. Roll a sausage to length. Pinch the sleeve at one end and pull downwards to lengthen one side. Pinch the sides of the widened sleeve and bring to a point.

14 Indent the centre of the sleeve with your finger, then bend the arm slightly. Add a few creases to the inside of the elbow using the sharp end of the leaf veiner.

15 Push the handle of a paintbrush into the cuff of the sleeve to create a space for the figure's hand. Twist and rotate to widen.

TOP TIP

Dip the paintbrush handle in corn flour (corn starch) before inserting into the sleeve, to prevent sticking.

16 Apply glue inside the hollowed sleeve and attach a hand. Glue the arm in position, applying glue to the inside of the sleeve, where it meets the cloak. Make sure the glue is tacky to the touch to prevent the arm from slipping out of place. Smooth and flatten the top of the shoulder slightly.

Repeat steps 13–16 for the other arm. With both in place, the hands can be brought forwards to almost touching. Push a cocktail stick into the neck of the model, trim to leave at least 1cm (½in) protruding.

17

Using 15g (½oz) of flesh-coloured paste, follow the instructions for making a head on pages 12–17. Paint the eye detail according to the gender of the model. Insert a cocktail stick up through the neck, into the head, to create a hole. Apply glue to the base of the neck then slide the head into position, taking care not to squash it out of shape. Leave the model to dry for a couple of hours.

Use the remaining black paste and roll a rectangle large enough to fit across the width of the upper part of the body. Cut a circle out of the centre of the rectangle using the wide end of a piping tip.

Cut along the longest sides of the rectangle to create neat, sharp edges. Hold the wide edge against the model to determine the finished width. The rectangle should be slightly wider than the shoulders. Cut off the excess on each side to suit.

Make a cut from the centre circle to the front wide edge of the rectangle to open. Colour 5g (1/6oz) of paste red. Roll it wide enough to fit across the length of the black rectangle. Cut four strips using a small strip cutter or, alternatively, cut freehand using a sharp knife.

Apply glue to the edges of the black rectangle and place each strip as shown, rolling each into position as it is placed, overlapping the strips in each corner. Trim away the excess.

Apply glue to the shoulders of the model. Using the cut in the rectangle to help you manipulate it, place the rectangle around the model's shoulders, placing the cut section at the front.

For the tie, roll a tiny ball of black paste and glue in position in the centre of the visible area of white shirt.

25 To make the collar, roll a small piece of white paste and cut a rectangle. Cut diagonally across the rectangle to leave two triangles. Flip one side over so that the two straight sides are facing each other.

26 Apply glue around the top of the tie and around the back of the neck. Attach each triangle with the straight edge positioned around the neck, as shown.

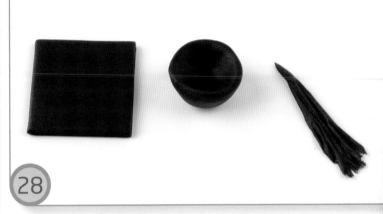

27 To make the ears, roll two tiny balls of flesh-coloured paste. Apply a small amount of glue where you wish to attach each ear. Push a paintbrush handle into each ball, press the ball onto each side of the head, then remove the handle. Indent the centre of the ear with a finger, or the paintbrush handle, and push back slightly to shape.

28 To create the cap, roll a small piece of the remaining black paste and cut a square. Roll a pea-sized amount of black paste into a ball and hollow into a 'cup' shape using a medium ball tool. Roll a long teardrop shape and flatten. Texture it with the sharp end of a leaf veiner then snip the wide end into a ragged shape to create a 'tassel'. Glue the upturned 'cup' to one side of the square, and the 'tassel' to the other. Set aside to dry while the hair is styled.

TOP TIP

If you stretch the hair too thin and gaps appear, simply add a flattened ball of paste to cover the gap. Dampen the tips of your fingers in water and gently smooth over the paste to eliminate the join. The paste will smooth easily and no one will ever know it has been layered.

29 Colour 5g (¹⁄₆oz) of fondant (sugarpaste) with chestnut colouring. Roll a ball and flatten into a circle almost big enough to fit around the back and top of the head. Apply glue to the head and attach the circle of hair. Apply gentle pressure and carefully stretch the hair into position using only the tips of your fingers. Work the paste around the neckline and forwards to just above the ears. Soften the front line of the hair.

30 Make sure the hat has dried before you glue it into position. Apply glue around the rim of the 'cup' and gently press onto the hair to secure it. Carefully position the 'tassel'.

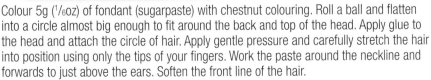

TIPS AND FINISHING TOUCHES

If you want, you can create additional details, such as the scroll. To make this, roll out some white paste and cut it into a small rectangle. Roll it up loosely and add a tiny strip of red paste as a ribbon. If you make this in advance and allow it to dry completely, you will be able to glue it onto an open hand without the scroll bending or curling out of shape.

To ensure that your model looks good from every angle, position the red-striped rectangle of paste carefully so that it hangs well and looks attractive.

With the cap in position, a small fringe can be added to the front of the hairline. Roll a tiny teardrop shape from chestnut-coloured paste and flatten it slightly, twisting to an upward point before gluing to the front of the head.

With a slight twist of the wrists when positioning the arms, you can manipulate the tiny fingers to almost interlock – support them with sponge as they dry, if necessary. The key is to use just a little glue when attaching the arms, so that it is tacky to the touch; too much glue and the arms will slide around.

As well as using kebab skewers in the legs, I would attach this figure to a cake with royal icing, just to make him extra secure.

63

Golden Wedding

This far-from-traditional topper captures the everyday romance of fifty years of commitment. I chose to accessorise the happy couple with tea and biscuits, but don't be afraid to adapt the design to your own needs. If you do decide to make a change, I would advise that you think about it carefully before you begin, and consider making prototypes of the accessories first, as they may affect the postion of the figures' arms and hands.

YOU WILL NEED

- 115g (4oz) black fondant (sugarpaste)
- 240g (8½oz) modelling paste
- 15g (½oz) fondant (sugarpaste)
- Autumn leaf, claret, dark brown, chestnut, ruby, ice blue, ivory and orange colouring pastes
- Sugar glue
- CMC (tylose) powder
- Rose, Cornish cream and white dusting powders
- Corn flour (corn starch)
- Small rolling pin
- Leaf veiner
- Small scissors
- Paintbrushes
- Small ball tool
- Medium ball tool
- Cutting wheel
- Stitching wheel
- Small piping tip
- Sharp knife
- Snippers
- Cocktail sticks
- Food-grade alcohol
- Icing (powdered) sugar

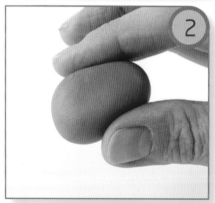

Make 115g (4oz) of black modelling paste: follow the instructions on page 8, using ready-made black fondant (sugarpaste) and ¼ tsp of CMC (tylose) powder. Use 110g (3¾oz) and set the remainder aside in a plastic bag. To make the trousers, follow steps 1–7 on pages 32–34.

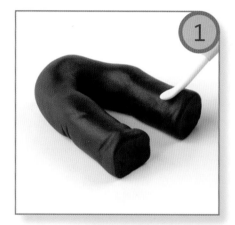

Colour 20g (¾oz) of paste with chestnut and orange colouring. To make the slippers, split the paste in two and roll each half into a ball. Place one ball into a plastic bag until ready to use. Roll a small sausage and flatten a little with your finger. Pinch in at the heel.

To mark the sole, indent around the edge of the bottom of the slipper using the sharp side of a knife. Work the line from the heel and all the way around the edge to end where you started.

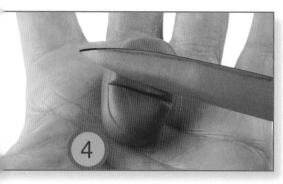

4 Indent the base of the slipper using the blunt side of your knife, to create the heel.

5 Pinch in at the heel to shape and open the indent a little.

6 Add some detail to the top of the slipper by criss-crossing the front with a stitching wheel. Repeat steps 2–6 to create the second slipper. Apply a small amount of glue to the top of each slipper and secure one to the end of each trouser leg.

7 To make the man's torso, colour 65g (2¹⁄₃oz) of paste with ice blue colouring. Take 45g (1²⁄₃oz) and set the remainder aside. Roll into a cone shape and flatten slightly.

8 Pinch around the bottom of the cone to widen and shape. Make a hollow in the centre with your fingers.

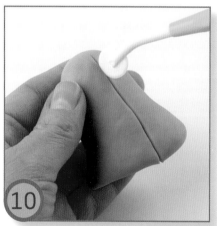

9 Using small, sharp scissors, snip a little way into the bottom of the shirt to open it slightly. Pinch either side of the cut to neaten and shape.

10 Add detail to the front of the shirt by running a cutting wheel from the cut line up to the neck.

11 Glue the shirt in position, smoothing the bottom edges down and around the top of the trousers.

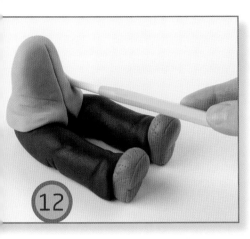

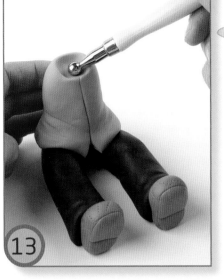

12 Indent the sides and around the bottom edge of the shirt with the wide, rounded end of the leaf veiner to create creases.

13 Work a medium ball tool into the neck area using small circular movements to widen and hollow.

14 Colour 80g (2⁴/₅oz) of modelling paste with flesh tones, see page 18. Take a pea-sized amount to make the neck and set the remainder aside.

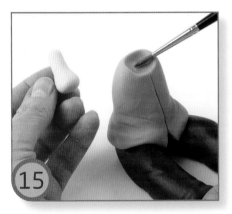

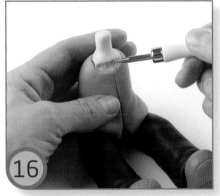

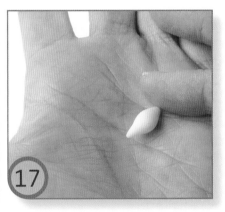

15 Roll a bean shape. Using a finger, roll out from the centre towards one end to lengthen it, keeping the other end rounded. Glue into position, smoothing the rounded end neatly into the hollow of the shirt.

16 To create the impression of a t-shirt, indent above the scooped neckline of the shirt into the flesh using the sharp end of a leaf veiner.

17 Roll a tiny sausage to fit the hollow created in the flesh, and roll to a point at either end.

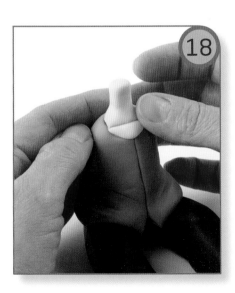

18 Glue the shape into position. Flatten and smooth with your fingers.

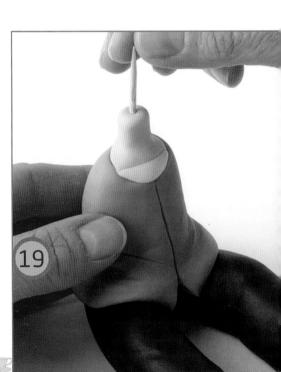

19 Push a cocktail stick halfway down into the body for support. Trim away any excess to leave at least 1cm (½in) protruding. Set the body aside to dry.

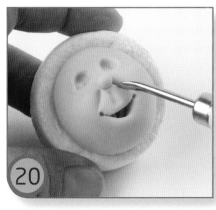

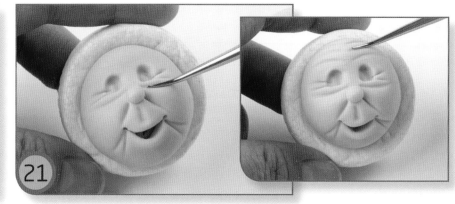

To make the head, use 16g (²/₃oz) of flesh-coloured paste and follow steps 24–30 on pages 37–38.

Add age lines around the mouth using the wider end of a metal leaf veiner. Carefully indent from the side of the nostrils down to the corners of the mouth, then indent the centre of the top lip. Add additional lines underneath each eye using the sharp end of the veiner. Push the tool into the paste and turn at a slight angle to create a slightly rounded indent. Mark the outer corners of the eyes with two small lines as shown. Finally, make a few lines across the forehead using the sharp end of the leaf veiner, working from the centre of the head towards the sides.

Add a small amount of blush colour to the cheeks: use a flat dusting brush to apply a mixture of rose dusting powder and icing (powdered) sugar. To create the eyeballs, follow step 31 on page 16.

To create eyelids, roll two tiny teardrops of flesh-coloured paste. Apply glue around the top and side of each eye and position the teardrops with the thick part on the inside of the eye, with the point curling around the eye. Use a dry, fine paintbrush to help smooth these in place.

Mix a little dark brown paste colouring with a few drops of alcohol until a smooth consistency is reached. Using a very fine brush, paint a line around the white of the eye, carefully painting under each eyelid. To create the pupils, follow the instructions on pages 16–17.

Use a cocktail stick to create a hole in the bottom of the head. Place the head in position on top of the neck without gluing, so that you can check the proportion. Trim the neck, if necessary, using scissors, then glue the head in position.

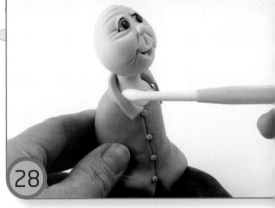

26 Roll a tiny piece of blue paste and cut buttons using a small piping tip. Glue four into position on the shirt, along the central line.

27 Roll a tiny strip of blue paste and cut a rectangle long enough to fit around the neckline of the shirt.

28 Place a small amount of glue around the neckline of the shirt. Position the rectangle so that one of its long sides runs around the neckline – the rectangle should be 'standing' up. Trim the front edges at either side so that they create a collar in the centre. Loosely fold down the collar, all the way around the neckline, using a leaf veiner or a paintbrush to assist you.

29 Adjust the paste with your fingers, curling the collar at the front to add character.

30 Make two hands following the instructions on page 19, and set them aside. Split 20g (¾oz) of blue paste in two and set aside one half. To make the right sleeve, roll the paste into a sausage, using the model to gauge the proportion. Indent the centre of the sleeve with your finger and bend the arm slightly at the elbow. Pinch the sides of the elbow to reshape, then apply some creases using the sharp end of a leaf veiner. Push a paintbrush handle into the cuff of the sleeve and twist to open. Apply glue into the sleeve opening and place the hand in position. Pinch the cuff to close over the wrist. Glue into position as shown.

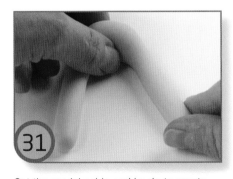

31 Set the model aside and begin to create the woman. Use 35g (1¼oz) of the remaining flesh-coloured paste. Roll into a long thin sausage. Bend in the middle to bring the legs together. Don't worry if the legs are slightly different lengths – simply trim them to size.

32 Pinch a little way in at the end of each leg to create part of the foot.
Hold the ankle between finger and thumb. Roll and stretch gently to taper. Flatten the foot and push forwards. Pinch around the heel and sole of the foot to sharpen the edge.

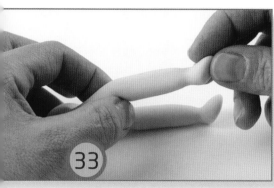

33

Indent the back of each knee with a finger to make a slight bend. The foot should only be half the size of its normal proportion as it will disappear into the slippers. If the foot is too long, trim the end with a knife.

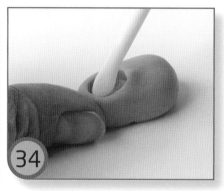

34

Colour 8g (1/3oz) of paste ruby. Pinch off a pea-sized amount and set aside. Split the remainder into two. Follow steps 2–5 on pages 64–66 to make a pair of slippers. Hollow the heel by pushing down into the paste with the wide end of the leaf veiner.

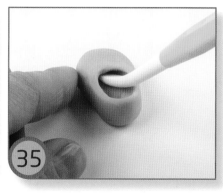

35

Scoop a little way forward into each slipper with the veiner, working back and forth to create a large enough hollow to fit a foot.

36

Apply a small amount of glue into the hollow of each slipper and insert the feet. Smooth around the seams with your fingers to reshape and neaten.

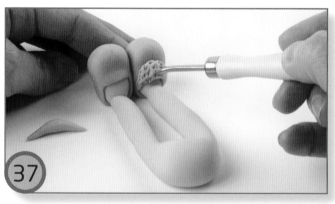

37

Use the pea-sized amount of remaining paste to make two tiny sausages, tapered at either end to fit across the front of the slippers. Glue into position and texture using the sharp end of the leaf veiner.

38

Colour 12g (2/5oz) of paste with chestnut colouring. Roll the paste and cut a semi-circle. Make the dome shape large enough to fit around the model's bottom, finishing with a straight line to fit just below the knee.

39

Create pleats along the length of the skirt using a paintbrush handle. Roll the handle back and forth firmly. Work along the width of the skirt leaving a little gap between each roll.

40

Turn the skirt over so that the inside is facing upwards. Turn the outer edge inwards, as shown.

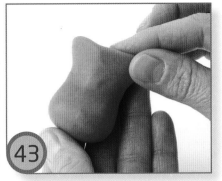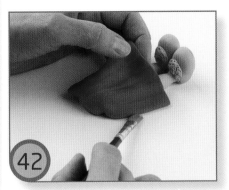

Apply glue all over the model's bottom and hips. Ensure the glue covers all the way to the work surface.

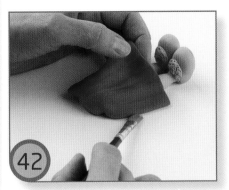

Flip the skirt over and attach the rounded end neatly around the bottom. Supporting the length with one hand, tuck the skirt around and under the hips using a dry, flat brush.

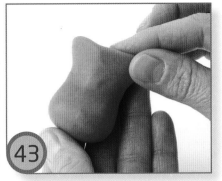

Colour 50g (1¾oz) of paste with claret colouring. Use 30g (1oz) to make the torso and set the remainder aside. Roll into a thick sausage. Roll across the centre of the sausage to indent the bust line. Pinch around the bottom edge outwards to widen and shape.

Glue the torso into position. Create a few creases at the bottom of the sweater and under the bust using the wide end of the leaf veiner.

For the roll-neck, roll a pea-sized amount of paste and flatten. Glue it in position. Make a slight hollow using a medium ball tool.

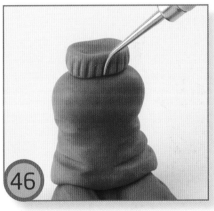

Use the sharp end of the leaf veiner to create a ribbed effect around the neck of the sweater. Push a cocktail stick half way down into the body for support. Trim to leave approximately 1cm (½in) protruding.

To make the head use 15g (½oz) of flesh-coloured paste. Follow steps 20–24 on page 68, adjusting the positioning of the black circles of the eyes to suit.

Apply glue to the neck of the sweater. Make a hole in the bottom of the head using a cocktail stick before twisting and pushing the head gently onto the supporting cocktail stick to ensure the pastes adhere.

(49)

(50)

To make the man's ears, roll two tiny balls of flesh-coloured paste. Push a paintbrush handle into each ball. Apply glue to the sides of the head and attach the ears, releasing the paintbrush. Indent the centre of each ear using the paintbrush handle and push slightly backwards.

To create the hair, mix 5g (¹/₆oz) of fondant (sugarpaste) with a tiny amount of black paste to make grey. Use about half of the grey paste, and roll a sausage long enough to fit across the back of the man's head from ear to ear.

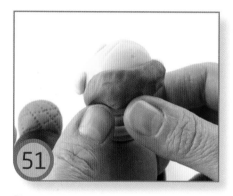

(51)

(52)

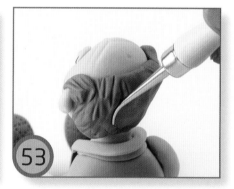

(53)

Pinch the bottom edge slightly to flatten, then glue the strip in position. Use the heat of your fingers to smooth and gently pull the hair into place.

Roll two tiny teardrops and attach one above each ear, with the pointed end towards the front.

Use the sharp end of the leaf veiner to add texture. Work in accordance with the hairline.

(54)

Roll two or three long teardrops of varying lengths from grey paste, and attach across the top of the head. Glue on one side, then drape the teardrop into position before gluing the other end.

Make the woman's hands and arms using 9g (¹/₃oz) of claret-coloured paste and a pea-sized amount of flesh-colured paste for each hand. Follow step 30 on page 69 to complete. Glue her left arm in position as shown. Arrange the models side by side with the male model sitting slightly ahead of the female. Allow enough space for the attachment of her right arm, which needs to stretch out and finish comfortably on his shoulder.

(55)

56

Make his left arm using the remaining 10g (²/₅oz) of blue paste set aside earlier. Follow step 30 on page 69 to complete. Glue his left arm in position as shown. Apply glue where the pastes meet to secure them.

57

Taking the right arm made in step 55, cut across the top of the shoulder and glue the arm in position. Apply a little glue to his right shoulder, where her hand will rest, and also to the inside of her arm where the pastes meet.

58

To create her hair, mix a tiny amount of black paste into 6g (¹/₅oz) of fondant (sugarpaste) to create a light shade of grey. Use half of the paste to roll a ball. Pinch it with your fingers to flatten and fit around the back of the head, then glue in position.

59

Roll teardrop shapes of varying sizes to fit around her hairline. Use the larger teardrops to add volume to the top and sides of the hair.

60

Texture using the sharp end of the leaf veiner. Work around the direction of the hairline and blend the teardrop shapes into the crown area.

61

Add a few small teardrops to the front of the hair, if necessary, to build volume and create random strands.

Using a shade of grey that matches the hair, roll two tiny teardrops and attach eyebrows to each model.

62

TIPS AND FINISHING TOUCHES

If you are creating your models to be placed on a cake later, it is important to allow them to dry completely before lifting them, as the connection between them is relatively weak. I recommend sliding a wide palette knife underneath the models to gently lift and place them, then secure with royal icing.

Use sponge to support the raised arm if it begins to slide when glued in position. Remember, that you only need a small amount of glue when attaching limbs – just enough to be tacky to the touch. This will dry much quicker than if you apply lots of glue, and the models will be more likely to hold their shape without any accidents!

Add a few little touches to complete your design. I used leftover paste to add a refreshing cup of tea and a few biscuits. Use small circle cutters for the saucer, plate and biscuits. For the biscuits you can colour a small amount of paste using ivory paste colouring or simply dust with Cornish cream dusting powder when the biscuits are made. Make a few random holes with the tip of a cocktail stick to complete.

The cup is made using a pea-sized amount of white paste rolled into a ball. Hollow the centre using a bone tool. Push into the ball and press the sides of the cup against your finger, working around the inside of the cup with the bone tool. Add a tiny strip of paste to the side: glue it to stand upwards and then curl it around to make the handle.

Why not embellish your design with a personal touch? You could create treasured possessions and gifts or even a favourite pair of slippers to make the cake extra special!

The small additional elements of the design should be left to dry completely before being attached to the models themselves. This will help the items to maintain their shape, and make the job of positioning them less fiddly!

Christmas

Father Christmas, Santa Claus or St Nicholas... Call him what you will, this jolly old man and his overflowing sack of presents make a great seasonal cake topper. Due to the weight of the hat and beard, it is crucial to allow the figure to dry out completely between stages, so that the body can withstand the additional weight without buckling or slumping. I used pre-coloured red fondant (sugarpaste) for this project, to ensure that I achieved a really vibrant, festive red.

YOU WILL NEED

- 215g (7²/₃oz) red modelling paste
- 35g (1¼oz) black modelling paste
- 135g (4¾oz) white modelling paste
- 15g (½oz) fondant (sugarpaste)
- Autumn leaf, claret, dark brown, chestnut and liquorice colouring pastes
- Sugar glue
- CMC (tylose) powder
- Rose, white and gold dusting powders
- Small rolling pin
- Leaf veiner
- Small scissors
- Paintbrushes
- Small ball tool
- Stitching wheel
- Piping tip
- Sharp knife
- Snippers
- Cocktail sticks
- Small pieces of sponge for support
- Pure, food-grade alcohol
- Miniature square cutter

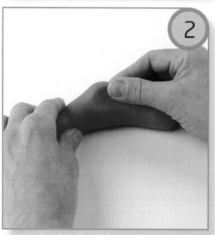

Make 215g (7²/₃oz) of modelling paste: follow the instructions on page 8, using ready-made red fondant (sugarpaste) and ½ tsp of CMC (tylose) powder. To make the trousers, take 90g (3¹/₅oz) of modelling paste and set aside the remainder. Roll the paste into a sausage. Leave the centre slightly thick and roll at either side to lengthen each leg to about three-quarters of the length of a full leg.

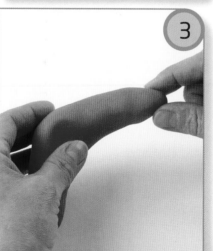

Pinch the centre of the trousers upwards a little to assist with supporting the body.

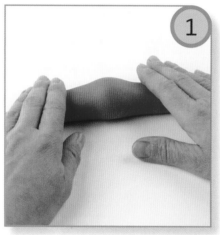

Indent behind each knee with a finger and bend a little. Roll the remaining part of the leg to a point.

4 Bend the legs so that they sit slightly apart. Indent the top of each thigh with the leaf veiner and pinch the centre to sit straight upwards.

TOP TIP

To strengthen small amounts of paste, leave a small pile of CMC (tylose) powder on a corner of your work surface, and dip the paste into the powder prior to use.

5 Use 12g (²/₅oz) of black modelling paste to make each boot. Roll a sausage and indent the centre by rolling back and forth with a finger.

6 Pinch the sausage forwards and flatten a little to shape and form the front of the boot. Smooth the sole of the boot with a finger.

7 Pinch around the edge of the sole to sharpen and define.

8 Push a paintbrush handle into the top of the boot. Rotate it firmly to open it out wide.

9 Place a finger inside the boot and pinch around the sides to thin them, stretching slightly as you work around the boot. Mark around the edge of the sole with a sharp knife. Indent the heel with the blunt edge of the knife to make the heel.

10 Apply glue inside the boot and position on the end of the leg. Twist the point of the leg into the boot to ensure the pastes adhere. Repeat to create and attach the second boot.

11

Use 70g (2½oz) of red paste to make the torso. Roll a fat sausage. Indent one side by rolling a finger back and forth. This will determine the bottom of the jacket.

12

Pinch around the bottom of the jacket to form a 'skirt'. Hollow out the centre using your fingers.

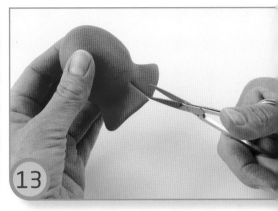

13

Snip the front of the jacket with scissors to open slightly.

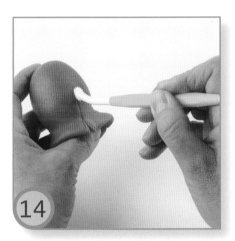

14

Add detail to the front of the jacket and around the bottom edge using a stitching wheel.

15

Glue the torso in position, with the top of the trousers fitting neatly into the hollow of the top as support.

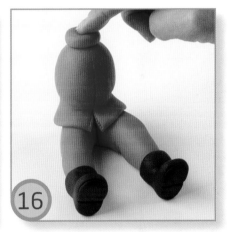

16

Use a pea-sized amount of red paste to create the neck. Roll a ball and flatten it. Glue it in position at the top of the jacket.

17

Colour 25g (⁹/₁₀oz) paste with flesh tones, see page 18. Following steps 24–26 on page 37, and using a big teardrop for the nose, create a face. Indent the nostrils using a small ball tool.

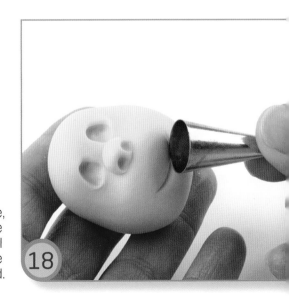

18

Use a piping tip to create a smile, leaving a wide space between the nostrils and the mouth. The space will look correctly proportioned once the moustache has been added.

19 Fill the eye sockets with tiny balls of white paste. To make eyelids, roll tiny teardrops of flesh-coloured paste to fit around the top of each eye. Make smaller, thinner teardrops to fit around the bottom of each eye. Glue the eyelids in place. Complete the eyes following the steps on page 17, but do not paint any lashes.

20 Push a cocktail stick into the body, at least half way down, leaving approximately 1cm (½in) protruding. Create a hole in the bottom of the head, then glue in position.

21 Cocktail sticks will be used to support the raised arms. In preparation, make a hole halfway into the shoulder area using a cocktail stick, at the angle that the arms will be positioned. Support the model with a piece of sponge propped against a solid background, to hold the model in a seated upright position without distorting the paste. Leave to dry overnight.

22 Make the gloves before making the arms. Use 3g (¹/₁₀oz) of black paste for each. Roll a teardrop shape and flatten gently with your finger. Pinch around the thin end to create a stalk-like wrist.

23 Cut a small 'V' on the side of the glove to indicate the thumb. Carefully pull the thumb outwards.

24 Flatten the hand a little more and smooth around the edge with your fingers. Smooth around the thumb to neaten and shape.

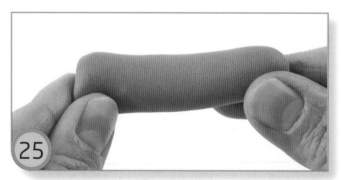

25 To make the sleeves, use 15g (½oz) of red paste for each. Roll into a sausage, using the model to gauge the proportion. Flatten the cuff end using a finger.

26 Flatten the top of the sleeve at a slight angle, this will allow the position of the arm to remain outstretched once it is glued in position.

80

27 Push a paintbrush handle into the cuff end of the sleeve and twist it gently to open up a hole. Apply a small amount of glue in the sleeve opening and place the glove in position. Pinch the cuff to close over the wrist.

28 Mark the inside of the elbow with the leaf veiner to create creases.

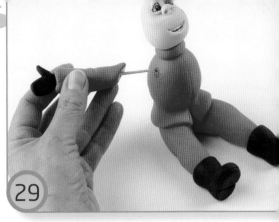

29 At the shoulder end, push a cocktail stick halfway into the arm, leaving approximately 1cm (½in) protruding. Glue around the shoulder area and insert the cocktail stick into the pre-made hole in the body. Twist a little to ensure the pastes adhere. Support the arms with sponge and leave the model to dry overnight.

30 Use some of the remaining flesh-coloured paste to make a button. Roll a tiny ball and flatten. Attach to the front of the jacket with glue.

31 Roll a small amount of black paste thinly. Use a knife to cut a strip to fit around Santa's waist.

TOP TIP

To cut the strip freehand, roll the paste and cut the length of the strip first, from the middle of the paste, then trim the top and bottom to remove a neat strip from the centre. Alternatively, use a strip cutter.

32 Apply glue around the waist of the jacket and attach the belt. Place the ends of the belt on top of each other and cut through both pieces for an even and neat finish.

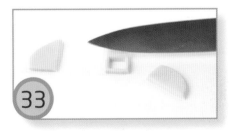

33 Make a tiny buckle using the remaining flesh-coloured paste. Roll the paste and cut a square using a miniature square cutter. Cut around the square hole with a knife to the thickness of the buckle you require. Glue in position at the front of the belt.

34 Make the beard using 9g (¹/₃oz) of fondant (sugarpaste). Roll it into a long teardrop, measuring it against the face to gauge the size. Pinch to flatten slightly, widening the paste to fit around the chin from ear to ear.

35 Texture the beard, working downwards along its length with the leaf veiner.

36 Apply glue around the chin and sides of the head and position the beard. Smooth the sides to blend the beard into the face. Retexture with the leaf veiner if necessary.

37 To make the hat use 20g (¾oz) of red paste. Roll a long cone shape with a definite point.

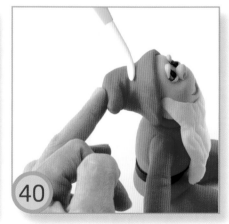

38 Pinch around the wide end of the cone to widen. Hollow the centre with your finger. Pinch around again to deepen the hollow enough to fit onto the head with ease.

39 Apply glue to the head and place the hat in position. Smooth the sides to ensure they adhere to the sides of the head. Bend the point to one side and smooth to shape.

40 Add a few crease lines to the inside of the hat fold using the wide end of the leaf veiner.

41 To make Santa's hair, use two pea-sized amounts of white fondant (sugarpaste), and roll into long teardrop shapes. Pinch and flatten with your fingers.

42 Attach each teardrop to the side of the head, with the wider end tucked just under the rim of the hat and the point trailing around to fit into the back of the neck. Pinch outwards so that the hair rests on the shoulder.

43 Roll a sausage of white fondant (sugarpaste) long enough to fit around the rim of the hat; pinch off the excess with your fingers. Glue the sausage into position.

44 Texture the paste using the sharp end of the leaf veiner. Push the tool randomly into the paste and flick swiftly to create a fur effect.

45 To make the moustache, roll two pea-sized amounts of white fondant (sugarpaste) into teardrops. Texture with the leaf veiner and attach each piece at either side of the top lip. Twist the points of the moustache to sit outwards. Roll a sausage of white paste to fit around the bottom edge of the jacket and finish it off as you did the hat. Make a tiny bobble for the hat using a pea-sized amount of white paste. Add a little texture before gluing into position and retexture if necessary once in place.

Use 100g (3½oz) of dark chestnut-coloured paste to make Santa's sack. Roll a ball and pinch around the top to create a lip. Hollow the centre with your finger. Pinch points at the bottom. Using about 10g (²/₅oz) of chestnut-coloured paste and a few tiny balls of black, copy the elements shown to create a tiny teddy bear.

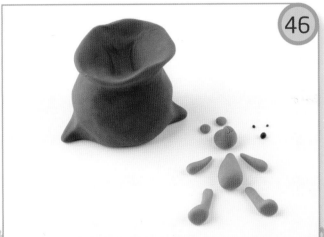

46

TIPS AND FINISHING TOUCHES

Texture over the joins in your fur trims on the hat and jacket, to ensure that they look like a seamless piece of paste.

It's important to allow drying time in between stages of making this model because of the additional weight of each step. Unless the model is being supported with a skewer through the body and into the cake or dummy cake, it is advisable to support the body with its head attached overnight, so that the weight of the hat does not pull the figure over. This will make life much easier when it comes to placing the model on top of its cake.

Mix a little gold lustre dust with alcohol and paint the button and buckle with a fine paintbrush. When you are using lustre colours to paint, always colour the paste to the nearest tone. Flesh or ivory is ideal for use with gold paint. Light or dark grey should be used for silver.

Create your own set of presents to fill Santa's sack. With the remaining pieces of paste, colour small amounts with your own choice of colour and cut into small cubes. Wrap a thin strip of paste around some to make a ribbon, and create bows for others, and you will have little parcels to add to the sack.

Happy 21st

Featuring a traditional 21st-birthday 'key to the door', this is the ideal cake topper for that landmark occasion. I chose to make the key from gum paste (flower paste), as the figure rests a hand on it, so it needs to be extra sturdy, while the fondant (sugarpaste) bow on top adds an extra girly touch! I tried to ensure that the figure's expression was a wide-eyed, open-mouthed look of excitement and happiness, so try to recreate this for yourself.

YOU WILL NEED

- 100g (3½oz) gum paste (flower paste)
- 160g (5²/₃oz) modelling paste
- 5g (¹/₆oz) black fondant (sugarpaste)
- 10g (¹/₃oz) fondant (sugarpaste)
- Autumn leaf, claret, dark brown, chestnut, egg yellow, navy, ruby and liquorice colouring pastes
- Confectioner's glaze
- Sugar glue
- Rose, white and antique silver dusting powders
- CMC (tylose) powder
- Small rolling pin
- Leaf veiner
- Small ball tool
- Medium ball tool
- Cutting wheel
- Stitching wheel
- Medium oval cutter
- Miniature square cutter
- Small piping tip
- Scissors
- Sharp knife
- Snippers
- Cocktail sticks
- Small blossom cutter
- Pure, food-grade alcohol
- Icing (powdered) sugar
- Corn flour (corn starch)
- Royal icing

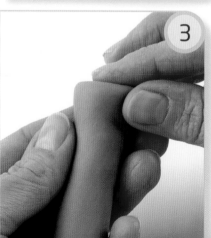

Make the key using 100g (3½oz) of gum paste (flower paste). Colour the paste with liquorice paste colouring to create a dark grey. Roll the paste to approximately 5mm (¼in) thick and use the template on page 128 to cut out the shape of the key. Use a medium oval cutter to cut out a hole at the top of the key, and miniature square cutters at the bottom.

Cut from the square holes to the edge of the key using a sharp knife. Leave the key to dry overnight on a sponge pad.

To make the legs, colour 60g (2¹/₁₀oz) of paste with navy colouring. Roll the paste into a sausage of the desired length and thickness. Pinch around each end of the sausage to sharpen and shape each hem.

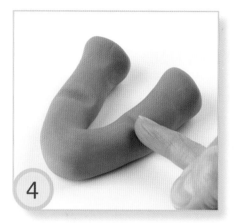

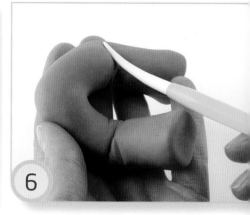

Bend the sausage in half to bring the legs together. Indent the back of each knee with a finger.

Bend each knee slightly, supporting the back of the leg with your hand and pushing your thumbs together at the knee.

Make creases on the back of the knees using the sharp end of the leaf veiner.

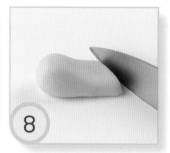

Colour 25g (⁹/₁₀oz) of paste with flesh tones, see page 18. Use 4g (¹/₆oz) for the feet and set the remainder aside. Split the paste in two. Roll each piece into a sausage and flatten at one end.

Cut along the flat end of each foot at a slight angle – cut each foot at a different angle to create a left and right. Smooth the cut line with your fingers to neaten.

Using the tip of the knife, make four small cuts along the flat edge of each foot. Make the first cut a little wider than the others to determine the big toe.

Use a small piping tip to make nail markings, being careful not to cut all the way through the tips of the toes.

To make the sandals, use a pea-sized amount of black paste for each – dip the paste into a small amount of CMC (tylose) powder to strengthen it before shaping. Roll a sausage to fit the length of each foot. Flatten with your finger.

Use the feet as a guide against the soles of the sandals. Pinch the paste as required making sure that for each shoe, the sole is a little wider than the foot.

Glue each foot onto its sole. Roll a tiny piece of black paste and cut a strip to fit across the front of each foot. Colour 5g (¹/₆oz) of fondant (sugarpaste) with ruby colouring. Roll a tiny piece and cut two small blossoms using a cutter. Glue one to the strap of each sandal. Set the rest aside.

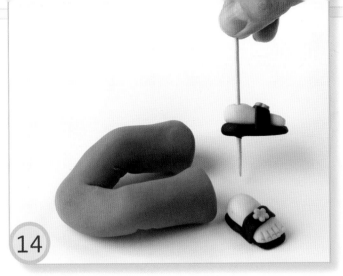

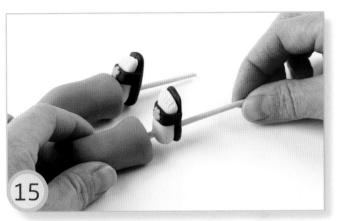

14 To avoid squashing the feet when you attach them to the trousers, push a cocktail stick through each to make a hole. Also make a hole halfway up into the leg from the bottom of the trousers, using a cocktail stick.

15 Apply glue around the bottom of the trousers and feed the cocktail stick through the bottom of the shoe and into the leg hole. Carefully press the shoes onto the trousers to adhere. Leave at least 2.5cm (1in) of the cocktail stick protruding, to support the figure when standing. Leave the legs to dry overnight.

16 Colour 55g (2oz) of paste egg yellow. To make the jacket, use 35g (1¼oz) and set the remainder aside in a plastic bag. Roll a thick sausage. Indent under the bust line by rolling back and forth with a finger.

17 Pinch around the bottom edge of the jacket to widen and shape. Make a hollow in the centre with your fingers.

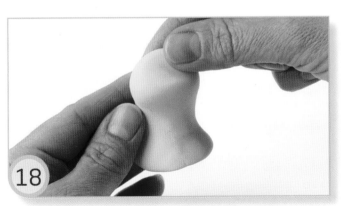

Hollow the top of the jacket using a medium ball tool.

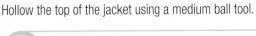

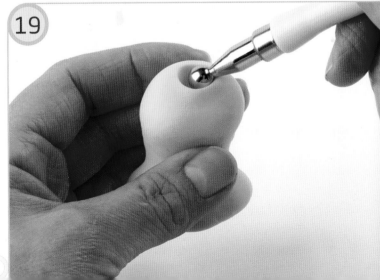

18 Pinch the top of the jacket almost to a point, shaping and smoothing the shoulder area with your fingers.

19

20 Pinch around the edge of the hollow, gently pulling upwards to stretch and make a collar.

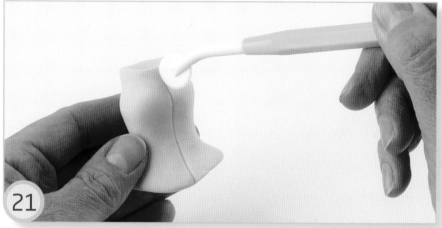

21 Detail the front of the jacket with a cutting wheel.

22 At the top and bottom of the line you just created, snip into the jacket with scissors, as shown.

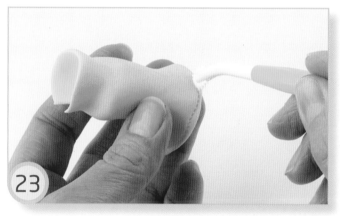

23 Detail around the bottom edge of the jacket using the stitching wheel.

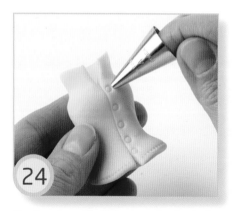

24 Create a line of buttons down the front of the jacket by pushing a small piping tip into the paste next to your vertical line.

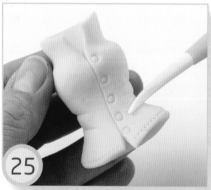

25 Add a few crease lines to the sides of the jacket, using the sharp end of the leaf veiner.

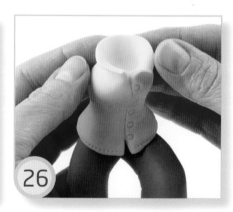

26 Stand the legs on a polystyrene dummy for support. Glue the torso in position, tilting it forwards slightly. Curl the edges of the collar downwards with your fingers.

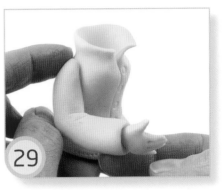

Colour 20g (¾oz) of modelling paste with flesh tones, see page 18. Set aside 15g (½oz) in a plastic bag and use the remainder to make the hands following the instructions on page 19. Set them aside while you make the sleeves. Roll 9g (⅓oz) of yellow paste into a sausage and measure it against the model to gauge the proportion.

Indent the centre of the yellow sausage with your finger and bend the arm slightly to create an elbow. Pinch the sides of the elbow to reshape. Push a paintbrush handle into the cuff and twist it to create an opening. Apply glue to the sleeve opening and place the hand in position. Pinch the cuff to close over the wrist. Repeat to create the second arm.

Glue the right arm in position as shown. Support with sponge until dry.

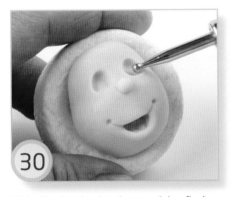

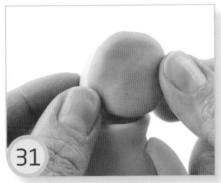

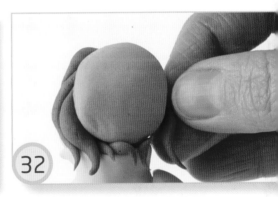

Make the head using the remaining flesh-coloured paste, following steps 24–30 on pages 37–38. To create the eyeballs, follow the instructions on pages 16–17. Glue the head in position and leave to dry for an hour or more.

Setting aside a pea-sized amount, use the remaining pink paste to make the beret. Roll a ball and flatten with your fingers to fit the back of the head. Detail around the edge with a stitching wheel.

Glue the beret in position on the back of the head. Colour 5g (⅙oz) of fondant (sugarpaste) with chestnut colouring. Roll small teardrops in varying sizes. Glue them in position around the beret to create a hairstyle.

For the top of the key, make a tiny bow with the remaining pink paste. Roll two small teardrops and a tiny ball. Glue the ball in position on top of the key and glue a teardrop on either side. Push a kebab stick into the cake to help support the key in an upright position. Attach the key to the cake using a little royal icing. Allow to dry. Mix silver lustre powder with alcohol to a thick painting consistency. Paint the key and leave to dry. Position the model on the cake, a little way behind the key, and secure with royal icing. Glue the left arm in position, as shown. Apply a little glue to the palm of the hand, and rest it through the handle of the key. Support with sponge until dry if necessary.

TIPS AND FINISHING TOUCHES

To add a bit of extra sparkle, when the key is completely dry, brush it with confectioner's glaze to add a shine.

To customise your figure, why not add a few more blossoms to the sandals or paint her toenails. Use powder colour mixed with a few drops of alcohol and a fine brush to apply. Powder colour will dry a little faster than paste colour. Any little extra detail will enhance the design, so have some fun with it!

The collar of the jacket gives extra support to the head once it is attached. I usually advise that you allow your model, with head attached, to dry overnight before adding a hat or hair, but this type of hairstyle – where only strands of paste are added to create a style – is simple and lightweight. Use your instinct to judge whether the model is strong enough to support the weight, and be patient if extra drying time is necessary.

Be sure to allow your key to dry completely before you position the model next to it – it could end up looking very patchy if you smudge it and have to touch up the paintwork.

93

Valentine's Day

Give a sugar heart to someone special this Valentine's day. Whether you create yourself or your loved one as the figure of this piece, be sure to make a gorgeous red heart as an accessory. Make the heart from gum paste (flower paste) to ensure that it dries quickly and forms a really sturdy shape.

YOU WILL NEED

- 70g (2½oz) red gum paste (flower paste)
- 80g (2⁴/₅oz) modelling paste
- 115g (4oz) black fondant (sugarpaste)
- Autumn leaf, claret, dark brown, ice blue, and liquorice colouring pastes
- Sugar glue
- Rose and white dusting powders
- Pure, food-grade alcohol
- CMC (tylose) powder
- Small rolling pin
- Leaf veiner
- Small ball tool
- Medium ball tool
- Paintbrushes
- Small piping tip
- Sharp knife
- Snippers
- Cocktail sticks
- Small pieces of sponge for support

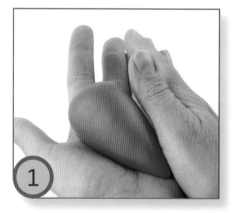

Use the template on page 128 or make a heart shape freehand, using 70g (2½oz) of red gum paste (flower paste). Knead the paste until warm and roll it into a large cone. Flatten with your hand and pinch the top sides to widen. Push a finger into the centre of the wide end of the cone to split the paste. Pinch and smooth around each side to round off the edges and shape to form a heart.

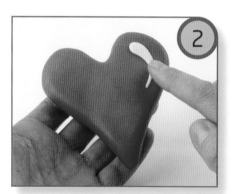

Roll a tiny teardrop of white paste and flatten. Glue into position on one side of the heart at an angle to imply light reflection. Set aside to dry.

Make 105g (3³/₄oz) of black modelling paste: follow the instructions on page 8, using ready-made black fondant and ¼ tsp of CMC (tylose) powder. To make the trousers and shoes, follow steps 1–8 on pages 32–35, substituting the coloured paste in the instructions with black. Finish off the shoes by marking around the bottom edge with a sharp knife to create the sole. Push into the heel using the blunt edge of the knife. Detail the bottom of the sole, marking a few lines with the knife. Glue in position. Add a little more detail to the trousers by gently pushing the rounded end of the leaf veiner into the paste to create creases and folds.

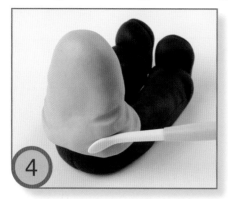

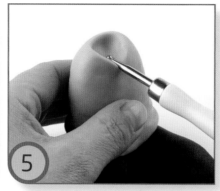

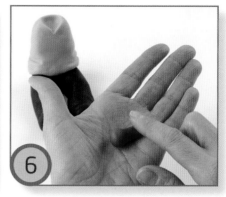

Colour 75g (2²/₃oz) of modelling paste ice blue. To make the torso, use 35g (1¹/₄oz) and set the remainder aside in a plastic bag. Follow steps 15–18 on pages 35–36 to create and attach it. Create folds and creases on either side of the waist using the rounded end of the leaf veiner.

Indent and hollow the neck using a medium ball tool. Pull the front of the neck down to a 'V' shape using the small ball tool. Soften around the edges with your finger.

Colour 16g (²/₃oz) of modelling paste with flesh tones, see page 18. To make the neck, take a pea-sized amount and set the remainder aside. Roll a bean shape then roll out from the centre towards one end with a finger, to lengthen one end, but keeping the opposite end rounded.

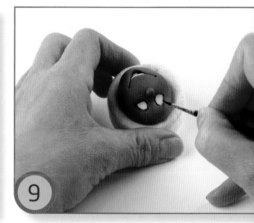

Glue the neck into position, with the rounded end fitting neatly into the hollow. Smooth around the join with your fingers.

Trim the neck to size, if necessary, with scissors. Push a cocktail stick down through the neck and halfway into the body for support. Trim the excess with snippers to leave about 1cm (½in) protruding.

To make the head, use 15g (½oz) of flesh-coloured paste and follow steps 24–30 on pages 37–38. To create the eyeballs, follow the instructions on pages 16–17. Use black paste colouring mixed with alcohol to paint around the eyes and add a tiny line for each eyebrow.

Push a cocktail stick up into the head to create a guiding hole. Apply glue to the head and neck, slide the head onto the supporting stick, and leave the model to dry overnight. Support against a piece of sponge in an upright position against a solid background, to prevent distortion of the paste.

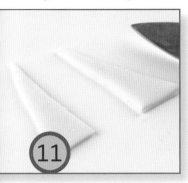

11

To make the collar, roll out a pea-sized amount of white paste and cut this into a small rectangle. Cut across the rectangle diagonally to make two triangles. Arrange the triangles on your work surface with the straight edges facing each other to resemble boat sails.

12

Apply a small amount of glue around the neckline of the shirt. Position the collar, attaching each straight edge around the neck as shown.

13

Make the hands following the instructions on page 19, using a pea-sized amount of flesh-coloured paste for each. Set them aside while you make the sleeves. Roll 8g (¹/₃oz) of ice blue paste into a sausage and measure it against the model to gauge the proportion. Indent the centre with your finger and bend the arm slightly. Pinch the sides of the elbow to reshape. Push a paintbrush handle into the cuff of the sleeve and twist it to create an opening. Apply glue into the sleeve opening and place the hand in position. Pinch the cuff to close over the wrist. Repeat to create the second arm.

14

Attach the model's arms at the shoulders with glue. Position the heart and secure with glue. Bring the arms forwards to make the hands rest at either side of the heart. Glue them in position on the legs. Use sponge to support until dry if necessary.

15

To create a hairstyle, roll 10g (²/₅oz) of black fondant (sugarpaste) into a ball. Pinch the paste to flatten and fit around the crown and top of the head. Glue in position. Using the tips of your fingers, gently blend the hair into place.

16

Work the hair around the sides of the ears and into the neckline, smoothing with your fingers.

17

Blend the front of the hair down onto the forehead, leaving a soft ridge across the top.

18

Pinch along the ridge to make peaks in the hair. Create the style to suit your needs.

TIPS AND FINISHING TOUCHES

Smoothing the hair around the head using the tips of your fingers is a simple way to create a style. I recommend that you leave ample drying time between adding a head and then applying hair, as it will create extra weight.

The model may appear to sit upright once it is complete but as it dries it may have a tendency to lean. Make sure you leave the model to dry overnight, with ample support behind it to maintain its stance, before you place it onto a cake.

If the hair shows any distortion or seams while styling, simply dampen your fingertips in water and smooth over the paste to blend. Any blemish or tear will soon disappear, leaving a perfectly smooth finish. This works best when using fondant (sugarpaste) without added CMC (tylose) powder.

There are cutters available for large shapes, but they are not always necessary. Freehand shaping is just as good if not better sometimes. I used gum paste (flower paste) to make my heart as it requires only a few hours to dry. Allow your piece to dry overnight if you choose to use modelling paste.

Bride and Groom

Make the cake the centrepiece of the celebration by recreating the happy couple in sugar: the dress, the suit, the flowers and the colours can all be brought to life here. Follow the basic processes given, but adapt the details as you need to. Due to the way the figures rest on the cake, you will need to create them in situ. For this reason, I advise you use a polystyrene dummy for the top tier of your cake, so that you can take as long as you like to perfect the figures, without worrying about the cake underneath.

YOU WILL NEED

- 420g (14⁴/₅oz) modelling paste
- 160g (5²/₃oz) black fondant (sugarpaste)
- 25g (⁹/₁₀oz) fondant (sugarpaste)
- Autumn leaf, claret, dark brown, ice blue, chestnut, red, green and liquorice colouring pastes
- Sugar glue
- Rose, white, silver lustre, gold lustre and pearl white lustre dusting powders
- Pure, food-grade alcohol
- CMC (tylose) powder
- Small rolling pin
- Leaf veiner
- Small ball tool
- Stitching wheel
- Paintbrushes
- Small piping tip
- Sharp knife
- Snippers
- Scissors
- Cocktail sticks
- Kebab sticks
- Small pieces of sponge for support
- Thin strip cutter (optional)

1 To make the base of the bride, use 100g (3½oz) of modelling paste and roll a thick sausage. This will form her 'legs'.

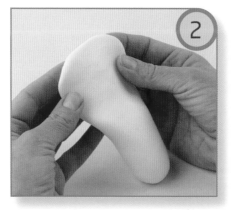

2 Flatten one half of the sausage with your hand. Pinch the flat edge outwards to widen, until the shape resembles a 'flipper'.

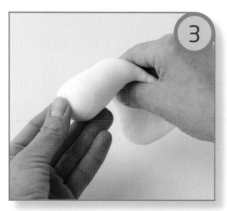

3 Bend the paste in the centre to form a 90-degree angle, so that the 'flipper' of paste hangs down. This part of the body will be hidden under the bride's dress so do not worry if the paste cracks a little, as it won't show.

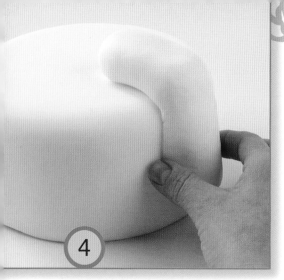

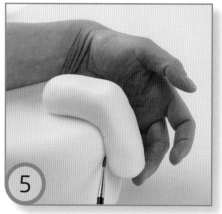

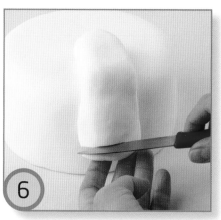

4 Position on the cake, as shown. Pinch in the sides of the 'flipper' of paste to make it bulge forwards. The top of the paste and the front should be a similar thickness.

5 Glue in position on the cake and also apply glue to the side edges to hold them securely in position.

6 Trim the bottom of the paste slightly to create a neat edge – it will need to be shorter in length than the skirt of the dress.

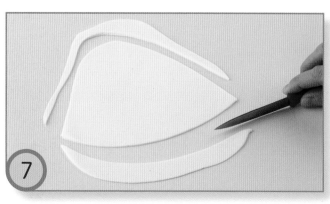

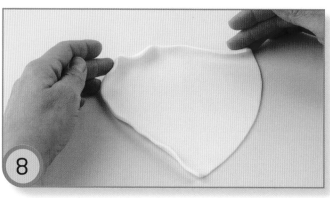

7 To make the skirt, roll 65g (2¹/₃oz) of paste thinly. Cut a shape with a curved top that will fit around and cover the thick, top part of the 'flipper', taking the knife wide to the sides to form a 'bell' shape that will form soft pleats when it drapes.

8 Turn the paste over so that the inside is facing up. Turn the sides and top of the paste inwards loosely.

Carefully lift the paste and attach from the top, smoothing the curled edges around the lower body shape with your fingers. Hold and support the opposite end of the paste to avoid the weight pulling the skirt down while you smooth it into position.

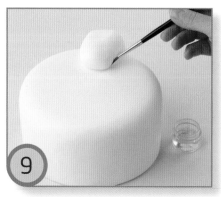

9 Apply glue around the top of the lower body shape, making sure that the glue reaches into the seam where it touches the cake.

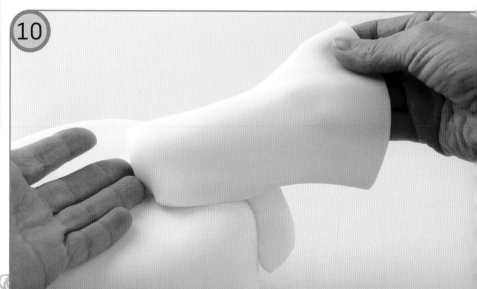

10

TOP TIP

The flat brush comes in particularly handy in this project, encouraging the paste into position without fear of distorting the cake covering or the model.

Use a clean flat dusting brush to tuck the paste firmly and neatly into the seams.

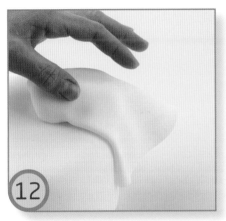

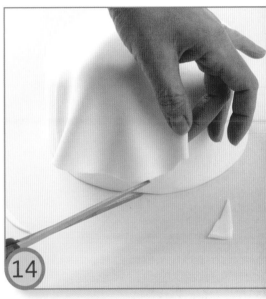

Fold the edges under along the entire length of the skirt, and carefully encourage the paste to lie in line with the 'legs'. Folds in the paste around the bride's bottom are acceptable. Smooth the paste gently without flattening it.

Push the bottom edges of the dress inwards slightly so that you can use the draped paste to create pleats. Encourage the shape and depth of each pleat by tucking a finger behind the paste and smoothing either side with your other hand as shown.

The centre of the skirt should be the longest part, so trim the sides with scissors if necessary. Trim from the centre of the dress towards the edges to shape, cutting only a small amount at a time. Apply glue to the cake where the sides rest and secure them in position.

To make the bodice, use 30g (1oz) of white modelling paste. Roll into a cone and flatten slightly.

Indent under the bust line with your thumb. Smooth and flatten from the bust line to the waist using your fingers.

Pinch the sides to shape, tapering in towards the waist.

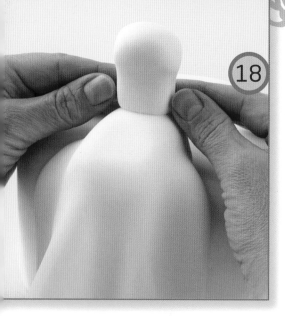

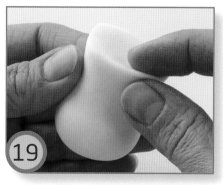

Cut across the bottom of the bodice to remove the rounded end. Place in position, on top of the skirt, without gluing, to gauge the proportion of the body. Bear in mind the shoulders have yet to be placed. The bodice should be slightly shorter than the distance between the model's bottom and knees. Trim any excess gradually from the bottom of the shape until the correct size is reached.

Pinch around the bottom edge of the bodice to make a 'skirt'. Hollow the centre of the paste with your fingers.

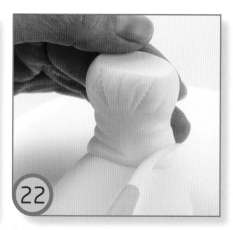

Cut across the top of the bodice to remove the rounded top. Detail the bust using the sharp end of the leaf veiner to add texture. Add a few lines using a stitching wheel.

Glue the bodice in position. Smooth the 'skirt' down onto the dress to fit neatly.

Add creases to the sides of the bodice using the sharp end of the leaf veiner, to create a ruched effect.

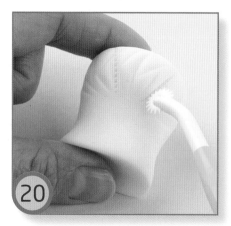

Colour 60g (2¹/₁₀oz) of modelling paste with flesh tones, see page 18. Use 6g (¹/₅oz) for the neck and shoulders, and set the remainder aside in a plastic bag. Roll a sausage to fit across the top of the bodice.

To make the neck, hold the paste in a pincer movement and gradually pinch around the centre of the sausage to form and stretch upwards to form a 'T' shape.

Cut across the bottom of the shoulders to leave a flat, straight surface, and glue in position on top of the bodice. Trim the neck to proportion, if necessary. Smooth and shape the shoulders with your fingers.

Push a skewer down through the neck and into the cake to secure. Be careful to check before pushing all the way into the cake that the skewer is straight and holding the model upright. Support the neck with your other hand while doing this. Trim the excess to leave about 1cm (½in) protruding. Reshape the neck after, if necessary.

To make the arms, take 14g (½oz) of flesh-coloured paste and split in two. Use each half of the paste to create an arm, following the instructions on pages 20–21. Attach the right arm to the body with glue, resting the arm on the lap, using pieces of sponge to support where necessary.

Glue the left arm in position as shown, with the hand resting on the cake. Smooth the seams between the arms and the shoulders with your finger. Apply a little glue under each hand to hold in place.

To make the head, use 15g (½oz) of flesh-coloured paste. Follow the steps on pages 12–17, giving the bride an excited, happy expression.

Trim the neck from the head. Push a cocktail stick halfway up into the bottom of the head, in preparation for attaching it to the body. Slide the head onto the skewer and gauge the proportion of the neck. Trim any excess, if necessary, before gluing the head in position.

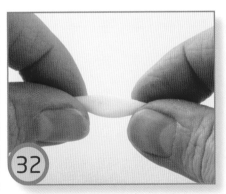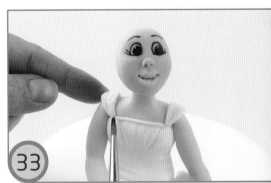

Roll two long, tiny strips of paste to fit across the seam at the front and back of the bodice. Glue in position.

To make the straps of the dress, roll two pea-sized amounts of paste into sausages. Twist either end to a point and flatten.

Add detail to match the bodice, using the sharp end of the leaf veiner and a stitching wheel. Glue the straps in place to hide the shoulder seams. Leave the model to dry overnight.

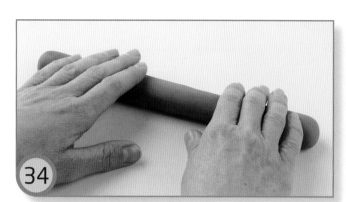

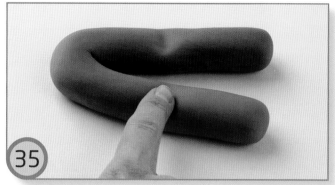

To make the groom's trousers, blend 100g (3½oz) of modelling paste with 30g (1oz) of black fondant (sugarpaste) to make grey. The mixture of the two pastes should be pliable enough to shape the trousers. If in doubt, dip the paste into a small amount of CMC (tylose) powder and knead well to strengthen. Roll a long, thick sausage.

Bend the sausage in half to bring the legs together. Indent the back of each knee with a finger.

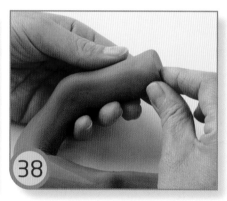

Bend the knees forwards. Reshape and smooth the sides of the trousers, keeping the width even from top to bottom.

To define the knee, support the leg with your hands and hold either side of the knee between your thumbs. Push your thumbs together, but without touching, to shape.

Flatten the bottom of each trouser leg with your fingers, and pinch around the edge to sharpen.

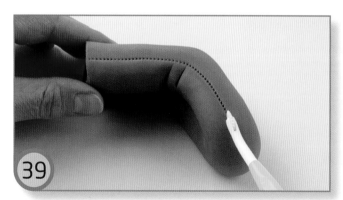

Run the stitching wheel along the outside and inside of each leg to add detail, and create creases behind each knee using the leaf veiner.

Glue the trousers in position – apply glue under the bottom and thighs, and a small amount on the back of the calves, and dangle the legs over the edge of the cake. Add a few creases to the bottom of the trousers using the flat end of the leaf veiner.

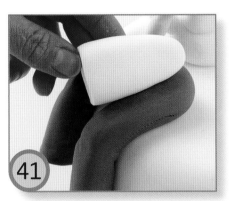

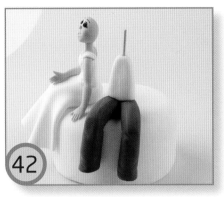

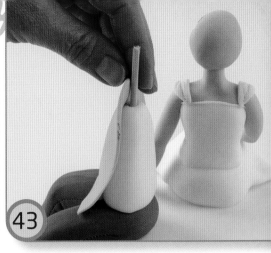

To make the torso, use 40g (1²/₅oz) of modelling paste. Roll it into a cone shape and flatten slightly. Measure the cone against the leg: to create the right proportion it should measure from the back of the trouser leg to the knee. Trim away any excess.

Glue the body in position on top of the legs. Push a skewer halfway into the body. Check the angle of the skewer is straight before making a final push down into the cake. Trim the skewer using the snippers, leaving about 1cm (½in) protruding.

To make the waistcoat, colour 6g (¹/₅oz) of paste with ice blue colouring. Roll a rectangle. To measure it, hold the shape against the front of the body, allowing it to overlap the trousers slightly at the bottom.

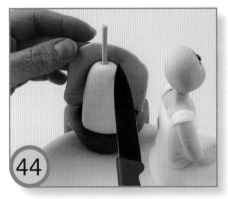

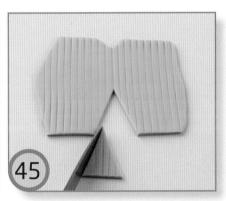

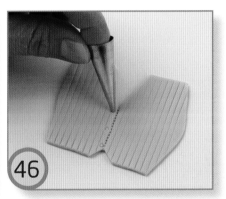

Use a knife or other tool to mark the back of the paste in line with the shoulders. Remove the paste from the cake and use your mark as a guide to trim away any excess.

Emboss the front of the paste with a small strip cutter. Cut a small 'V' up from the bottom centre of the paste. Cut another 'V' down from the top, in line with the smaller one, to about halfway down the front.

Detail the front centre with a stitching wheel. Add button detail using a small piping tip pushed into the front of the waistcoat.

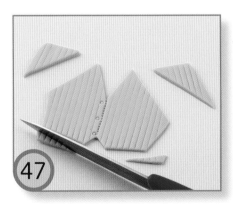

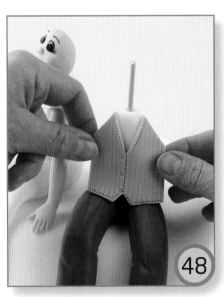

Trim the bottom of the waistcoat at either side at a slight angle, as shown. Trim at an angle from the top of the neck to the outside edges and discard the excess.

Detail the edges with a stitching wheel. Hold the waistcoat against the body to ensure the length and size is correct. Ensure you have a slight overlap at the bottom, to hide the join from the body to the trousers. Don't worry if the top points are slightly short of the shoulders, as they will be hidden by the jacket.

49

Apply a little glue to the top sides of the body and place the waistcoat in position. Smooth the sides to blend with the body. Leave a little room at the front of the waistcoat so that it hangs comfortably.

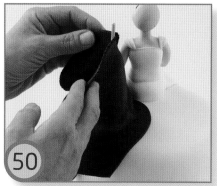

50

Make 110g (3¾oz) of black modelling paste: follow the instructions on page 8, using ready-made black fondant (sugarpaste) and ¼ tsp of CMC (tylose) powder. To make the jacket, take 50g (1¾oz) and set the remainder aside in a plastic bag. Roll the paste wide enough to wrap around the model. Cut a straight edge along the bottom of the paste, and place it around the shoulders of the model with 1cm (½in) overlapping the cake.

51

To determine how long the jacket should be, mark the inside of the jacket in line with the shoulders, using a knife. Remove and lay the paste flat on your work surface, then cut across the top using this marking as a guide. You now have the finished length of the jacket to work with.

52

Either use the template on page 128, or cut the shape freehand, as follows. With the inside of the jacket facing, mark a line down the centre with a knife, being careful not to cut all the way through. Use this line as a guide to shape the jacket.

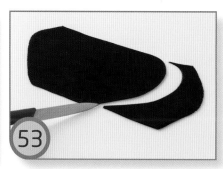

53

Cut the paste into a curving shape: at the top, measure 4.5cm (1¾in) from your centre line, and from this point cut a curving shape that swoops around and meets the centre line at the bottom.

54

Fold the trimmed side over loosely and use as a template to cut the other side to match. Lay it flat and reshape the point at the bottom with a knife, if necessary.

55

Cut a little way into the pointed paste. This will allow the coat tails to splay open when placed in position.

Without gluing, wrap the jacket around the shoulders to gauge the width. The front should be left open enough to see the waistcoat underneath. Remove the jacket and trim any excess before securing it around the shoulders with glue.

56

Open the front of the jacket slightly and glue the insides to hold the sides of the jacket in position. Leave slightly open at the front.

To create the bride's hair, colour 15g (½oz) of fondant (sugarpaste) with chestnut colouring. Use three-quarters of the paste and roll it into a ball. Set the remainder aside. The ball should be just slightly smaller than the bride's head.

Flatten the ball with your fingers and pinch to shape around the back of the head. Stretch the paste so that it finishes below one cheek and sweeps around to finish on the opposite shoulder. Any excess can be pinched off and set aside. Glue across the top and around the back of the head. Position the paste as shown, leaving the sides loose.

Texture the hair with the sharp end of a leaf veiner. Create sweeping lines across the back of the head.

Add texture to the inside of the loose hair hanging at either side, being careful not to mark the face.

Make space for the ponytail by trimming the bottom of the paste resting on the right shoulder.

Roll half of the remaining paste into a teardrop shape. Flatten slightly and texture with the sharp end of the leaf veiner. Glue in position with the point facing downwards.

Use the remaining paste and roll teardrops of varying sizes. Add texture and attach to the front and sides of the hair. Twist the ends to a point and shape when in position.

Add a few single strands to complete the style. Use the leaf veiner to make little adjustments.

109

66 Make the groom's hands following the instructions on page 19, using a pea-sized amount of flesh-coloured paste for each. Set them aside while you make his sleeves. Follow step 13 on page 97 to make the sleeves, using 25g (⁹/₁₀oz) of black paste for each instead of blue. Cut the top of each shoulder at an angle on the inside of each arm. Glue in position. Rest his left hand on his lap, and rest his right hand on top of the bride's left hand.

67 To make the groom's head, use 16g (²/₃oz) of flesh-coloured paste and follow the instructions on pages 12–17. Trim the neck slightly, if necessary. Insert a cocktail stick through the neck and about two-thirds of the way into the head, before gluing in position on the skewer. Twist firmly but gently into the neck area to ensure the pastes adhere.

68 To make the groom's tie, mix a tiny amount of black paste into a pea-sized amount of white paste to create a light grey. Roll into a teardrop and flatten slightly. Texture with the sharp end of the leaf veiner. Trim the top of the teardrop, and cut the pointed end with scissors, snipping from the front of the tie down and towards the back.

69 Glue the tie in position with the point fitting into the top of the waistcoat. Leave a small gap showing at the top of the tie to make room for a knot. Roll a tiny sausage of paste and flatten slightly. Texture with the leaf veiner and place across the top of the tie as shown.

70 To make the jacket lapels, roll a small amount of black paste. Cut a strip to fit around the back of the neck and down the front of the jacket at either side.

71 Cut each side of the lapels at an angle. Apply glue to the front edge of the jacket and position the lapels to hide the edge.

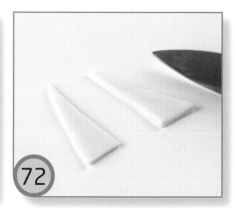

72 To make the collar, roll a pea-sized amount of white paste and cut it into a small rectangle. Cut across the rectangle diagonally to make two triangles. Arrange them on your work surface with the straight edges facing, so that they resemble boat sails.

73

Apply glue to the top of the tie and around the jacket collar. Position the shirt collar, attaching the straight edge of each piece around the neck, as shown.

74

To make the groom's hair, colour 10g (²/₅oz) of fondant (sugarpaste) with dark brown colouring. Pinch the paste to flatten and fit around the crown and top of the head. Glue in position. Using the tips of your fingers, gently blend the hair into place, working the hair around the sides of the ears and into the neckline. Smooth with your fingers. Blend the front of the hair onto the forehead, leaving a soft ridge across the top (see finished photograph for reference). Pinch along the ridge to make peaks in the hair. Create the style to suit your needs.

75

Roll a tiny amount of flesh-coloured paste very thinly, and cut a tiny strip to fit across the groom's wedding finger. Use a damp glue brush to pick it up and position it. Flatten the brush between your fingers, and use the straight, damp edge to tuck the tiny strip into the finger creases.

76

To make the shoes, use 10g (²/₅oz) of black modelling paste for each. Follow steps 8–12 on page 46. Glue each foot in position and place a piece of sponge underneath to support it until dry.

To make a single rose, colour a pea-sized amount of modelling paste red. Roll the paste thinly. Press your finger onto the paste along one side and pull outwards to create a scalloped line of petals. Roll the paste, gathering firmly along the straight edge but keeping the petals fairly loose. When you have finished rolling, fold the petals outwards with the tip of your finger or a dry paintbrush. Pinch off the excess with your fingers. A stalk and leaves can be made from thinly rolled strips of green paste.

77

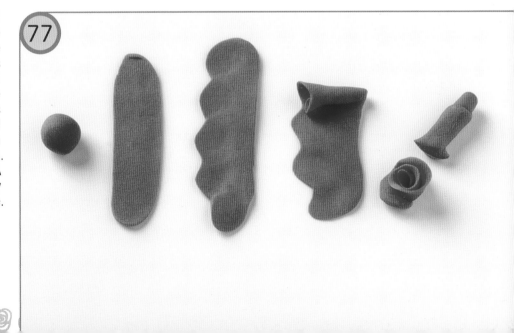

TIPS AND FINISHING TOUCHES

The happy couple! The models aren't sitting too close together but close enough to still be speaking. I purposely do this to make it easier to dress the models, and to create them in stages allowing for drying time. When you gain more confidence in making these models, you will be able to judge the positioning to suit yourself, and manipulate the paste without hesitation.

One single rose is a nice touch. Make the flowerhead as per step 77, then add a tiny amount of green paste rolled into a thin sausage for a stem, along with tiny flattened teardrops as leaves. You could eliminate making the bride's hand altogether and cover it instead with a small triangle of white paste. Use a small blossom or daisy cutter to cut lots of tiny flowers and cover the entire triangle to create a bouquet.

Any detail added to the back of the bride's dress which requires using a stitching or cutting wheel should be done when the paste is newly placed in position. Once the paste has dried, this kind of detail would not be possible. Add buttons and bows once the figures are complete. All the little personalised additions make this your own.

Hairstyling is a fun part of making models. This is where your own creativity takes over. The key is to use fondant (sugarpaste) without the addition of CMC (tylose). Remember also, that you don't have to texture the hair using a tool. Smooth hair is just as pretty, and the paste is easy to manipulate into position using the tips of your fingers. Any tears in the paste are easily sorted by rubbing over the area with a little water on the tip of your finger. Build up the volume by blending more paste onto the head and smoothing out the seams in the same manner. Add little blossoms to the hair to finish off.

It is very sweet if the models end up sitting the way you had originally planned in your head. Sometimes this isn't the case, as the body of one may be positioned a fraction differently to your original plan and there's nothing you can do about it once it is secured. When I place the arms on the models, I allow the model to show me where the hand will rest on its own in a comfortable position and I make my final decision to glue or not to glue in place.

Mix a little silver lustre powder with alcohol and paint the tie to give it a satin sheen. Use the tip of a fine paintbrush to colour the buttons. Mix gold lustre powder with alcohol and use a fine paintbrush to colour the wedding band.

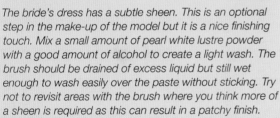

The bride's dress has a subtle sheen. This is an optional step in the make-up of the model but it is a nice finishing touch. Mix a small amount of pearl white lustre powder with a good amount of alcohol to create a light wash. The brush should be drained of excess liquid but still wet enough to wash easily over the paste without sticking. Try not to revisit areas with the brush where you think more of a sheen is required as this can result in a patchy finish.

I create all of my wedding couples on dummy cakes covered in fondant (sugarpaste). This allows me ample time to get the models done in time for the wedding without worrying about the date of expiry for the cake involved. It also makes a memorable keepsake that can be easily removed from the cake without causing damage. I attach a cake card to the bottom of a dummy of the same size and cover with fondant (sugarpaste). Leave to dry for at least 24 hours before creating the models. The top tier of the cake can be complete in advance and it makes life a whole lot simpler. I make my toppers up to two weeks in advance and store on a cool, dry shelf.

113

Indian Wedding

This gorgous, easy-to-personalise cake is the perfect finishing touch at any wedding. As for the other wedding cake on pages 100–113, I would advise you to use a polystyrene dummy for the top tier of your cake. Allow ample drying time between the steps on these models. I often add the hair to a male model on the same day as the head has been attached, but if you want to create hair that is a little longer, I would recommend that you leave the head to dry for longer beforehand.

YOU WILL NEED

- 500g (1lb 1oz) modelling paste
- 170g (6oz) red modelling paste
- 20g (¾oz) black fondant (sugarpaste)
- Autumn leaf, claret, dark brown, chestnut, caramel/ivory and liquorice colouring pastes
- Sugar glue
- Rose, white and gold lustre dusting powders
- Pure, food-grade alcohol
- CMC (tylose) powder
- Small rolling pin
- Leaf veiner
- Small ball tool
- Scriber needle
- Large and small stitching wheels
- Cutting wheel
- Small circle cutter
- Paintbrushes
- Small piping tip
- Sharp knife
- Snippers
- Scissors
- Cocktail sticks
- Kebab sticks
- Small pieces of sponge for support
- Royal icing

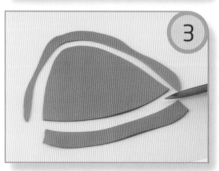

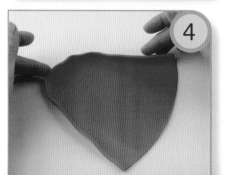

1 The base of the bride's body and sari is made in the same way as the dress for the Bride and Groom cake; follow steps 1–6 on pages 100–102.

2 Make 170g (6oz) of red modelling paste: follow the instructions on page 8, using ready-made red fondant (sugarpaste) and just over ¼ tsp of CMC (tylose) powder. Roll 60g (2¹/₁₀oz) of the paste thinly and set the remainder aside in a plastic bag.

3 Cut a shape with a curved top that will fit around and cover the thick, top part of the lower body shape made in step 1, taking the knife wide to the sides to form a 'bell' shape that will form soft pleats when it drapes.

4 Turn the paste so the underneath is facing up. Use your fingers to gently turn the sides and top of the paste inwards loosely. Leave the wide, bottom edge unturned.

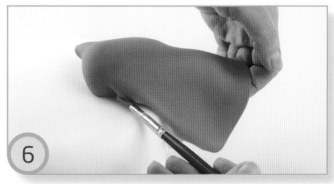

5 Apply glue around the top half of the lower body shape, making sure the glue reaches into the seam where it touches the cake. Carefully lift the red paste and attach from the back, smoothing the curled edges around the lower body paste with your fingers. Hold and support the other end of the red paste to avoid the weight pulling the dress down while you smooth it in position.

6 Use a clean, flat dusting brush to tuck the paste firmly and neatly into the seams. Fold the edges under along the entire length of the skirt, and carefully encourage the paste to lay in line with the 'legs'. Folds in the paste around the bride's bottom are acceptable. Smooth the paste gently without flattening.

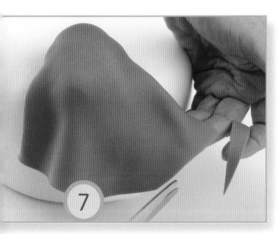

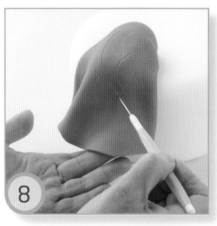

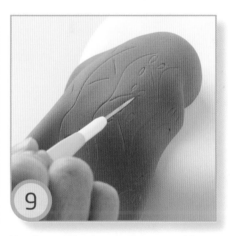

7 The centre of the skirt should be the longest part, so trim with scissors if necessary. Trim from the centre of the dress towards the edges to shape, cutting only a small amount at a time.

8 Carefully pull the bottom of the dress forwards slightly and support underneath with one hand. Use the scriber needle to detail the dress with the pattern given on page 127.

9 Use the needle at an angle so as not to tear the paste. When making oval shapes with the needle, do this in two halves: a small angled stroke of the needle to one side joined by another on the opposite side. This prevents the paste from tearing.

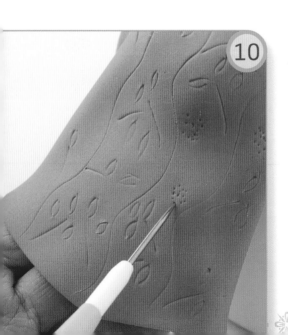

Pushing the needle in clusters of dots will give the appearance of flowers once the painted detail has been applied. Tuck the sides of the dress neatly under using a dry, flat brush to finish off.

Roll 60g (2¹/₁₀oz) of red paste thinly. Cut a dome as before (step 3) and turn over so that the inside of the dome is facing up. Turn the edge of the paste inwards along the right side only.

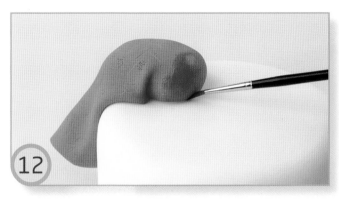

12 Use a small paintbrush to apply glue carefully to the back of the bride's bottom.

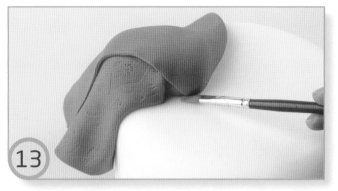

13 Attach the red dome to the seated model at an angle, so that the straight edge runs straight down the front of the dress, and the skirt spreads out across the cake to the left of the figure. Use the flat brush to smooth and neaten the back of the dress, tucking the edge under.

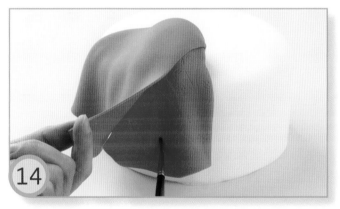

14 Apply glue underneath the top layer and rest the top in position without flattening it.

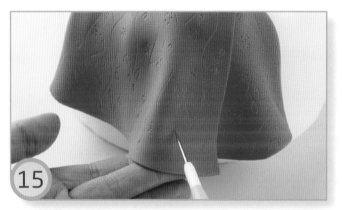

15 Detail the front panel of the dress as before in steps 8–10, using your hand to support the paste underneath.

Push the left side of the dress inwards slightly so that you can use the draped paste to create pleats. Encourage the shape and depth of each pleat by tucking a finger behind the paste and smoothing either side with your other hand as shown.

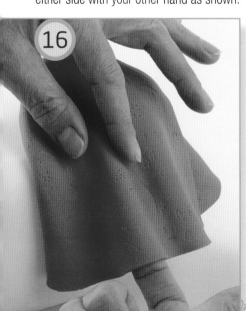

16

17 Colour 90g (3¹/₅oz) of modelling paste with flesh tones, see page 18. Use 35g (1¹/₄oz) for the torso, and set the remainder aside in a plastic bag. To make the bride's torso, roll the paste into a cone and flatten slightly.

18 Create a neck at the wide end of the cone, pinching all around to smooth and lengthen it.

117

19

Indent under the bust with your finger, then smooth and flatten from the bust line down to the waist. Pinch the sides to shape them, tapering the shape inwards towards the waist.

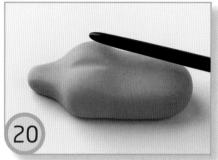

20

Indent the centre of the bust using a paintbrush handle.

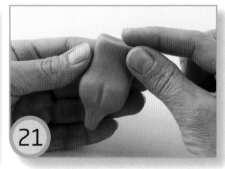

21

Cut the rounded end from the bottom of the torso to leave a clean flat finish. Sit the torso on the model to gauge the proportion. Pinch around the bottom edge to widen and soften.

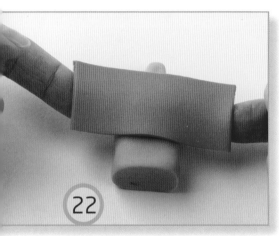

22

To make the top part of the dress, use 5g (¹⁄₆oz) of red paste and roll thinly. Cut a rectangle large enough to fit across the bust, finishing at either side of the body.

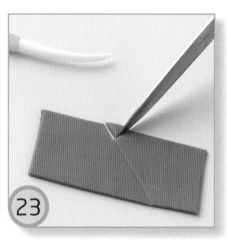

23

For added detail, mark a diagonal line across the centre of the rectangle. Cut a small 'V' shape at the top, as shown.

24

Detail as in steps 8–10, using the scriber needle. Glue the piece in position, resting on the bust. Smooth around the sides to neaten them.

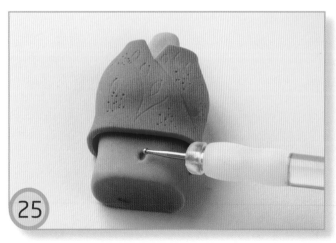

25

Create a tummy button using the smallest ball tool. Push in gently and pull downwards a little.

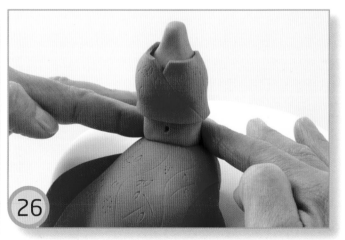

26

Glue the torso in position, smoothing the edges into the dress with your fingertips.

118

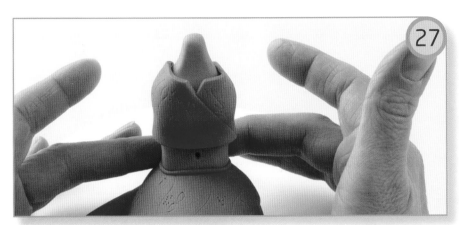

Roll a tiny strip of red paste and glue this around the seam to hide the join between the torso and the skirt, if necessary. Make sure the join is at the back of the figure.

Secure the model by pushing a skewer down through the neck, through the body and into the cake. Trim using snippers, leaving approximately 1cm (½in) protruding. Reshape the neck if necessary.

To make the arms, use 7g (¼oz) of flesh-coloured paste for each, and follow the instructions on pages 20–21. Use pieces of sponge to support where necessary. Glue the arms in position as shown. Smooth the seams with your finger. Apply a little glue under each hand to secure.

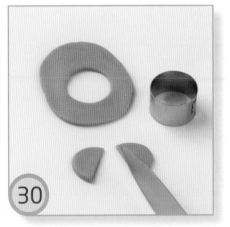

Roll a small amount of red paste and cut a small circle using a circle cutter or the wide end of a piping tip. Cut the circle in half to make two capped sleeves.

Pinch the straight edge of a semi-circle sleeve to widen it so that it will fit around the top of an arm. Glue in position with the rounded end attached to the shoulder. Tuck in at the seams with the help of a dusting brush. Repeat for the other sleeve.

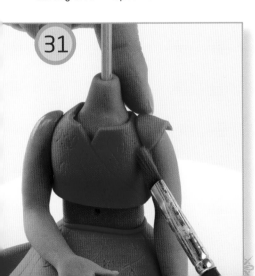

To make the head, use 15g (½oz) of flesh-coloured paste. Follow the instructions on pages 12–17, hollowing the eye sockets into elegant almond shapes, as shown. Fill with teardrops of white paste and flatten.

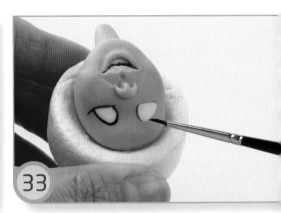

Mix a little dark brown paste colouring with a few drops of alcohol until a smooth consistency is reached. Paint around the eyes, following the line of the eye as shown.

119

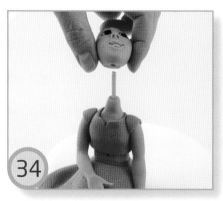

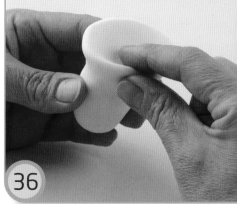

34 Trim the neck from the head. Push a cocktail stick halfway up into the bottom of the head, in preparation for attaching to the body. Slide the head onto the skewer and gauge the proportion of the neck. Trim any excess, before gluing the head in position. Leave to dry overnight.

35 Colour 300g (10²/₃oz) of modelling paste ivory. Use 130g (4²/₃oz) to make the trousers and set the remainder aside in a plastic bag. The groom's trousers are made in the same way as for the Bride and Groom cake; follow steps 34–40 on page 106.

36 To make the torso, use 45g (1²/₃oz) of ivory paste. Roll into a cone shape and flatten slightly. Gauge the proportion against the model, as in step 41, page 107. Pinch around the bottom edge to widen. Hollow the inside with your fingers so the shape will fit neatly on top of the trousers.

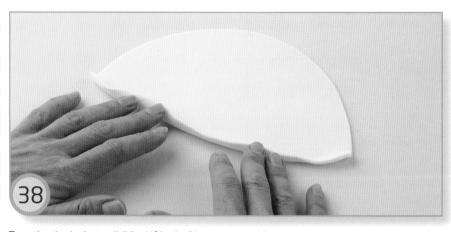

37 Glue in position. Smooth the paste onto the front of the legs, and at the sides and back. Push a skewer down through the body and into the cake. Trim with snippers to leave approximately 1cm (½in) protruding.

38 To make the jacket, roll 50g (1³/₄oz) of ivory paste wide enough to wrap around the model. Cut a straight edge along the bottom of the piece and hold it against the back of the model, with the straight edge overlapping the cake by about 1cm (½in). Mark the piece about 2cm (¾in) above the shoulders and remove from the cake. Use your mark to judge the length of the jacket, cutting the piece into a wide semi-circle. Gently turn the straight edge over.

Glue the jacket onto the body across the back of the shoulders, leaving the excess at the top resting against the skewer. Turn the bottom edge inwards to rest neatly against the model.

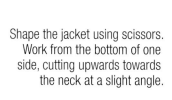

Shape the jacket using scissors. Work from the bottom of one side, cutting upwards towards the neck at a slight angle.

41

Cut around the neck to remove the excess paste. Follow around the other side of the jacket with the scissors, trimming to shape. Turn the bottom edge inwards allowing the jacket to hang loosely. Secure at the neck and inside each side of the jacket with a little glue.

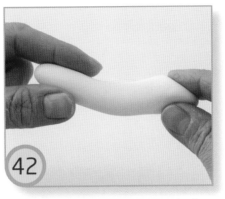

42

Make a pair of hands using a pea-sized amount of flesh-coloured paste for each. Follow the steps on page 19. Set the hands aside while you make the sleeves. Use 25g ($^9/_{10}$oz) of ivory paste for each sleeve. Roll a sausage to length and bend slightly in the middle. Pinch the sleeve at the front and pull downwards to create a flared end. Pinch the sides of the widened sleeve and bring to a point.

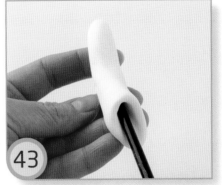

43

Indent the centre of the sleeve and bend the arm forwards a little more. Add a few creases to the inside of the elbow using the sharp end of the leaf veiner. Push the handle of a paintbrush into the cuff of the sleeve. Twist and rotate to widen the opening. Apply glue to the hollowed sleeve of each arm and attach each hand.

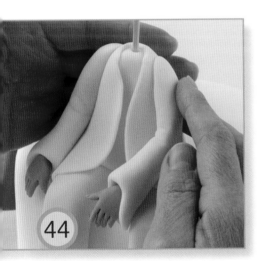

44

Glue the arms in position as shown, with the right hand resting on the cake and the left arm across the model's lap. Smooth the shoulder seams.

45

Mix chestnut paste colouring with a little alcohol until a smooth consistency is reached. Paint the henna detail onto the bride's hands and arms using the tip of a fine paintbrush. A series of lines and little dots is enough to create the impression of this pretty paintwork.

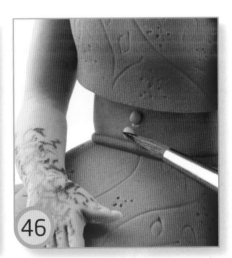

46

Roll two or three tiny balls of flesh-coloured paste and attach onto the tummy button as shown. Use a glue brush to lift and place in position.

47

Roll a small amount of flesh-coloured paste. Score about eight parallel lines in the paste using a cutting wheel, being careful not to cut all the way through.

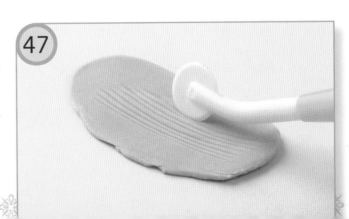

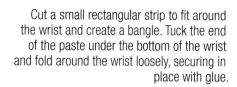

Cut a small rectangular strip to fit around the wrist and create a bangle. Tuck the end of the paste under the bottom of the wrist and fold around the wrist loosely, securing in place with glue.

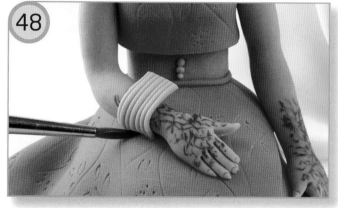

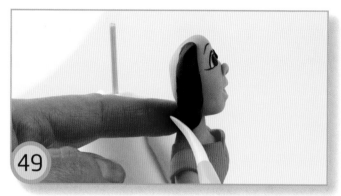

To style the hair, use 5g (¹/₆oz) of black fondant (sugarpaste). Roll two teardrops of slightly different lengths. Attach the rounded end of the first teardrop to one side of the top of the head, to create a side parting, and trail the thin end around the side of the face to rest at the back of the neck. Texture using the leaf veiner.

Apply the second teardrop, shaping it round the face as before, and carefully texture the paste while in position. Indent the paste around the edges to create a wavy style.

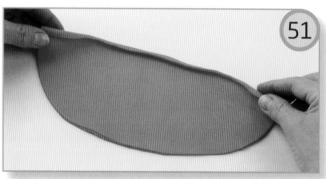

To make the shawl, use 50g (1¾oz) of red paste. Roll into a rectangle large enough to fit around the top of the head, with either side of the shawl resting just below each arm. Cut a straight line across the top. The shawl should rest on the cake with enough overlap to turn inwards for a neat finish – cut at an angle around the bottom to the correct length.

Glue in position across the top of the head. Apply glue to the top of the arms to secure the shawl in place.

Use a small amount of flesh-coloured paste to create the chain jewellery. Roll thinly and make a line using a large stitching wheel. Cut along either side of the stitched line to leave a thin detailed strip.

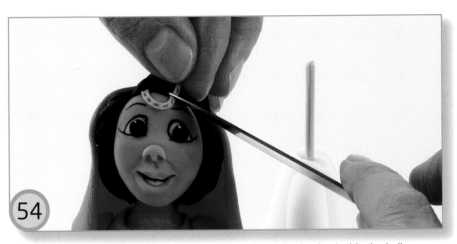

Create two hollows in the hairline using a small ball tool. Apply glue inside the hollows. Insert one end of the tiny strip into one side. Trim the other side to size and tuck the end into the remaining hollow.

Repeat the same and add a chain from the nostril to the side of the head.

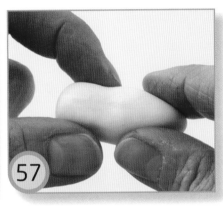

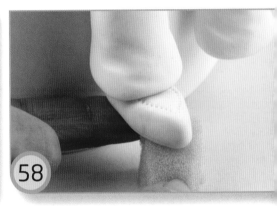

To make the groom's head, use 16g (²/₃oz) of flesh-coloured paste and follow the instructions on pages 12–17. Trim the neck slightly, if necessary. Insert a cocktail stick through the neck and about two-thirds of the way into the head, before gluing in position on the skewer. Twist firmly but gently into the neck area to ensure the pastes adhere. Roll a small amount of ivory paste. Cut a small rectangle to fit around the neck; glue in an upright position around the neckline.

Use 10g (²/₅oz) of ivory paste to make each shoe. Roll a sausage and flatten slightly. Pinch in at the ankle and at the front of the shoe, as shown. Mark the bottom edge of the shoe to create the sole using a sharp knife.

Indent the heel using the blunt side of the knife. Add detail to the top of each shoe using a small stitching wheel. Glue in position at the bottom of each trouser leg and support underneath with sponge until dry.

To make the hair, roll 10g (²/₅oz) of black fondant (sugarpaste) into a ball. Flatten and pinch to shape around the top and back of the head. Pinch downwards at the bottom to add extra length. Texture the shape with the sharp end of the leaf veiner.

Glue the hair in position. Use the tips of your fingers to gently stretch the paste into position. Roll varying sizes of teardrops – attach them all over the head to create volume and style. Retexture with the leaf veiner where necessary.

123

TIPS AND FINISHING TOUCHES

Mix bold gold lustre powder with alcohol and use a fine brush to paint all the jewellery. The effect will be quite stunning.

Powder colours mixed with alcohol will dry quicker and have a more subtle appearance than paste colours, and are ideal for lips. I don't always paint the lips on the models. Often I will simply brush inside and around the mouth with rose powder colour, and the effect is just as pleasing.

The shawl can add quite a weight to the model. Make sure that she has been left to dry overnight before applying. The shawl may appear to sit perfectly well at that moment, but as it settles and dries it will gradually pull the head back. Patience during drying times will pay off.